KT-558-101

S

John

dvanced

icMaster

Series

Eric Ma

Philip Allan Updates
Market Place
Deddington
Oxfordshire
OX15 0SE

Orders
Bookpoint Ltd, 130 Milton Park, Abingdon, Oxfordshire, OX14 4SB
tel: 01235 827720
fax: 01235 400454
e-mail: uk.orders@bookpoint.co.uk
Lines are open 9.00 a.m.–5.00 p.m., Monday to Saturday, with a 24-hour
message answering service. You can also order through the Philip Allan
Updates website:
www.philipallan.co.uk

Printed in Spain

Environmental information
The paper on which this title is printed is sourced from mills using wood from
managed, sustainable forests.

Contents

Introduction

In 1989 the Communist Party states in eastern Europe collapsed. There were powerful popular demonstrations in Czechoslovakia and the German Democratic Republic and in November 1989 the Berlin Wall was breached and pulled down. To many it seemed like what the French Revolution must have felt like about 100 years earlier: a tidal wave of liberation sweeping away authoritarian regimes that had appeared to be set in stone and destined to last, if not for ever, at least for the foreseeable future.

The collapse of the Communist Party states was seen at the time as a crisis not just for Marxism, but for socialism in general. British politicians like Margaret Thatcher proclaimed socialism to be dead. The following year the USSR changed dramatically as countries within the old Soviet system broke away and declared their independence, and the USSR became the Russian Federation. Even Leningrad reverted to its pre-revolutionary name of St Petersburg.

Although socialists in general and even most Marxists had long distanced themselves from the Communist Party states, these regimes described themselves as countries of 'real existing socialism' and there is no doubt that the revolutions of 1989 cast doubt upon the whole socialist project. The idea of trying to socialise the market to any degree seemed doomed, and those who argued that socialism was unworkable and at least implicitly totalitarian appeared to have been vindicated. Communist parties in East and West changed their names — usually to insert 'democracy' in the title — and a book by Francis Fukuyama, an American scholar, posed the question as to whether liberal capitalism was the regime of the future and the model towards which all systems were inevitably tending.

Socialism is a particularly diverse kind of movement and one of the aims of this book is to explain the extraordinary variety of socialism, or 'socialisms' as Tony Wright called his work (1996). Socialism may take antagonistic forms and in Chapter 1 an attempt is made to define socialism in general, to see whether it is possible to locate some kind of unity within this diversity. Particular attention is paid to the problem of utopia, since all socialism is vulnerable to the argument that it assumes a fanciful concept of human nature and its project is hopelessly unrealistic. This is why a whole chapter is devoted to the claim that socialism can be presented 'scientifically' rather than as some kind of 'utopian' doctrine; Chapter 2 attempts to explain why Marxists see other varieties of socialism as 'utopian' in character.

Utopia is not the only problem that besets socialism. Marxism in particular is subject to a view of history that is not only implausible, but has authoritarian consequences. Moreover, the notion of class struggle as the way to achieve socialism seems problematic, as does the idea that morality is a 'bourgeois' notion that socialists should repudiate. Chapter 3 argues that the notion of 'scientific socialism', as espoused by Marxists, leads to an authoritarian society that discredits socialism itself. Is democratic socialism or social democracy an improvement? The work by the German socialist Eduard Bernstein is examined. Bernstein came out of a Marxist tradition and his critique of classical Marxism evoked a storm of protest from the orthodox; it is a pioneering text of what came to be called 'social democracy'.

Chapter 5 examines the development of the Labour Party in Britain, a party that, unlike the German Social Democratic Party, was never influenced by Marxism and sees itself as a pragmatic and constitutional party. Does the Labour Party in Britain reveal a problem of identity — the problem that it is so realistic that it appears indistinguishable from liberal or even one-nation conservative parties? This problem is looked at with particular reference to Blair's leadership and philosophy. The critics of socialism take the view that socialism, in whatever form, interferes with human freedom and necessarily makes unacceptable inroads into the market, so that whatever it claims, it is indeed a 'road to serfdom', as Hayek entitled one of his celebrated books.

The final chapter assesses whether socialism can be rescued from its problems. It suggests that if we draw upon the strengths of the social democratic *and* Marxist traditions while seeking to discard their deficiencies we can come out with a socialism that is both realistic and utopian, sensible and yet radical.

John Hoffman

Acknowledgements

I am very grateful to Eric Magee for his help and advice. I have also found that writing and editing for *Politics Review* has been a huge help in writing this work. Philip Allan Updates has been a wonderful publisher to work for, and I hope that our association will long continue.

I am very grateful to Edinburgh University Press for permission to draw upon work that I have done for a *Glossary of Political Theory*.

Rowan Roenisch has been encouraging and helpful, as have my daughter, Frieda Roenisch, and my son, Fred Hoffman.

Socialism or socialisms?

Socialism is certainly a broad church and it embraces a bewildering variety of doctrines and movements. But it is not infinitely elastic and I will try to argue that it is an ideology of the 'left' rather than of the 'right'. Some movements have called themselves (or they have been called by others) socialistic, although in the view taken here they cannot be regarded as socialism. Nevertheless, the definition offered of socialism is very inclusive and it seeks to suggest that all socialisms have something in common. The question of utopia deserves a special mention since socialism's critics charge it with being unrealistic and fanciful, and the term 'utopian' is often used to capture its deficiencies.

The problem of variety

It is revealing that Tony Wright calls his book *Socialisms* (1996), and he does this in order to emphasise the plurality of approaches and doctrines that make up the socialist movement. Not only is the term elastic, but it covers movements that contradict and contest one another.

Some socialists are religious, others doggedly atheistic in character. Some advocate revolution, others reform. Nor will socialisms with one characteristic necessarily have the others. Authoritarian socialisms may be atheistic (as in the Communist tradition) but they need not be. Saddam Hussein's Baathist regime has been likened to the USSR under Stalin (1879–1953), but it is noteworthy that Hussein claimed adherence to some kind of Islamic tradition.

Some socialists, like Tony Benn (1925–), admire the role of Parliament because they believe that Parliament represents the voice of the popular masses, while other socialists may stress the importance of Parliament as a bulwark against radicalism. Still others see parliamentary democracy as an obstacle to socialist advance.

Marxism and social democracy

The distinction between Marxism and social democracy is the major fault line among socialisms. The term 'social democracy' will be used throughout this book interchangeably with 'democratic socialism', although this is controversial with those Marxists who believe that only a socialism based upon soviets or workers' councils is truly democratic.

Illustrated London News

Lenin and Stalin, 1922

The history of socialist thought is thick with accusations of betrayal. Lenin (1870–1924), who led his Bolshevik Party to victory in 1917, believed that social democrats were traitors to socialism because they supported the First World War and opposed the Russian Revolution. Socialists influenced by libertarian or anarchist ideas felt that Lenin and the Bolsheviks betrayed the Soviet experiment by crushing the rebellion of Bolshevik sailors that took place in Kronstadt (in the USSR) in 1921.

Others placed the authoritarian 'deviation' later in time. Trotsky (1879–1940), one of the organisers of the Russian Revolution and a key figure in winning the civil war, felt passionately that Stalin had reneged on the revolutionary traditions of Lenin by seeking to build socialism in one country and introducing a tsarist-type style of leadership and politics, while Mao Zedong (1893–1976) and many Chinese Communists believed that the Russians had surrendered to capitalism and the market after 1956. The Russian Communists were denounced as 'revisionists' and armed skirmishes actually took place between China and the USSR in the late 1960s.

The British Labour and Communist parties

The differences discussed above have deeply divided socialists. Marxists themselves have fractured into warring groups and even the adherents of Trotsky have been subjected to intense schisms. Social democrats are divided from Communists, and the British Labour Party, for example, repeatedly refused the request for affiliation from the Communist Party of Great Britain (CPGB) on the grounds that the latter supported dictatorship and not democracy. Communists and left-wing democratic socialists were considered threats to the German constitution even when German socialists were in office in the old Federal (or West) Germany. The social democratic version of socialism has been particularly strong in Britain.

Mention has already been made of the way in which Communists have been deeply divided (as in the armed conflict between the Soviet Union and the People's Republic of China in the 1960s), but reference can also be made to the intervention of Vietnam into Cambodia or Kampuchea in 1978. It should not be forgotten that when the Warsaw Pact intervened in Hungary in 1956 and Czechoslovakia in 1968, it was Communists who were pushed out. Their ideas and policies seemed threatening to the USSR because they sought to reform the political and social system of their particular country. Western Communists influenced by social democratic and liberal ideas called themselves 'Eurocommunists'. They denounced the Soviet Union and eastern European Communist Party states as 'totalitarian' in character, and were in turn called 'revisionists' and 'traitors' by the defenders of orthodoxy.

The differences between social democracy and Marxism are set out in Table 1.1.

Table 1.1 Differences between social democracy and Marxism

Social democracy/democratic socialism	Marxism/scientific socialism
Moderate classes	Eliminate classes
Utilise the state	Go beyond the state
Parliament	Workers' councils
Ethically desirable	Historically inevitable
Nation as a whole	Workers and their allies
Evolutionary reform	Revolutionary seizure

The differences between orthodox Communists and their left-wing critics are set out in Table 1.2.

<table>
<tr><td>Table
1.2</td><td colspan="2">Differences between orthodox communism and its left-wing critics</td></tr>
</table>

Orthodox communism	Left-wing critics
Existing states (now only Cuba, China, Vietnam and North Korea)	Systems in the future — none at present
Party has a leading role (constitutionally enshrined)	Party based on real popular support
Carefully selected legislature	Soviets or workers' councils
Marxism as the official doctrine	Marxism as a popular ideology
Tightly controlled media	Open and critical media
Salary differentials based on party-endorsed criteria	All paid the same

Defining socialism

Bernard Crick, in his book *In Defence of Politics* (first edition 1963), sees conservatives, social democrats and liberals as exponents of politics, a process that Crick defines as an activity seeking to conciliate and compromise. He contrasts advocates of politics with nationalists, Communists and extremists of various kinds. Crick regards himself as a democratic socialist and he is sharply critical of Marxism. Nevertheless, despite the argument that certain kinds of socialists have more in common with liberals and conservatives than with the ideas of other socialists, we shall locate the common features of all socialists in terms of the following:

- **An optimistic view of human nature.** Humans are changeable and they can become more sociable. Human nature, as it currently exists, does not constitute a barrier to social regulation or ownership. The contention that humans are too selfish to cooperate and to have common interests contradicts socialist doctrine.
- **A stress on cooperation.** All socialists take the view that people can and should work together. This means that the market and capitalism should be replaced by the community, or at the very least the market and capitalism can, and should be, modified in order to facilitate cooperation. Competition may be seen as an aid to, or wholly incompatible with, cooperation, but the latter is the guiding principle.

- **A positive view of freedom.** Socialists feel that the question of freedom must be examined in a social context and therefore freedom is more than the right to act without deliberate, external interferences. Freedom for socialists requires resources of a material kind. The right to read and write, for example, involves the provision of schooling if such a right is to be meaningful.
- **Support for equality.** Socialists define equality in dramatically different ways: some see it merely as equality of opportunity and respect, others argue that it requires the distribution of resources so that all have the same amount. But all socialists must subscribe to equality in some form or other. This, as Crick argues in *Socialism* (1987), is 'the basic value in any imaginable or feasible socialist society'.

What socialism excludes

The above characteristics explain why socialism, although a broad church, is not infinitely elastic. Dr Verwoerd (1901–66), the architect of South Africa's system of apartheid, was sometimes accused by his free-market critics of being a socialist, since the apartheid system involved extensive state controls and interference with the market.

Indeed, the Nazi Party described itself as a party of 'national socialism' (as we shall see in the case study), but in the case of both this and apartheid, extensive state control and interference with the market was based upon explicit hierarchies that socialism rejects, in theory at any rate. The Nazi Party espoused doctrines of racial superiority and elitism that are anti-socialist in character: the commitment to socialism by some fascist theoreticians is propagandist in character and not genuine.

Socialism is a broad church: it stretches from Pol Pot (1925–97) to Tony Blair but it cannot incorporate those who specifically and deliberately reject the notion of equality. It may be that for the inmates of a concentration camp or the victims of genocidal slaughter, there is not much difference between the oppression of the 'right' and the oppression of the 'left', but the point is crucial. Socialists have sometimes committed terrible violations of human rights but they have done so in the name of equality and emancipation. These are not concepts that appeal to ideologues of the extreme 'right'.

There is a further characteristic of socialism that is more contentious: utopianism.

The problem of utopia

All socialists are vulnerable to the charge of utopianism — of trying to realise a society that is contrary to human experience and historical development. Socialists disagree as to whether utopianism is a good thing or a bad thing. In his famous book on the subject, *Utopia*, Thomas More created the notion of a good society ('eutopia') that is nowhere ('utopia' = 'no place'). Karl Mannheim (an interwar German sociologist), in *Ideology and Utopia* (1936), defined utopia as an idea that was 'situation transcending' or 'incongruent with reality': it 'breaks the bonds of the existing order'.

While some socialists have seen utopia as a good thing, liberals and conservatives regard the notion of utopia as negative — an irresponsible idealism that rides roughshod over the hard facts of reality so that utopianism can at worst lead to nightmarish regimes of a highly oppressive and totalitarian kind. Heywood, in his book *Political Ideologies* (1992), argues that all socialists are utopians since they develop 'better visions of a better society in which human beings can achieve genuine emancipation and fulfilment as members of a community'. He even extends this to Marxism, where he describes communism as 'a utopian vision of a future society envisaged and described by Marx and Engels'. On the other hand, he acknowledges that the issue is controversial, since he also notes that Marx and Engels supported 'scientific socialism' and rejected what they called 'utopian socialism'.

Can utopias be realised?

Geoghegan, in his *Utopianism and Marxism* (1987), declares himself 'in praise of utopianism', although he concedes that utopians have often been 'unrealistic', 'irrational', 'naïve', 'self-indulgent', 'unscientific', 'escapist' and 'elitist'. But does this mean that socialism can never be realised?

Geoghegan seems to be saying that utopianism is an 'ought' that is in opposition to an 'is', so that liberals and conservatives can argue that utopians support ideals that can never become part of social reality. However, it is not clear from Geoghegan's argument as to whether socialist utopianism is an 'ought' permanently at war with an 'is', or whether the problem lies with the critics of utopianism who are guilty of what he calls a 'sad dualism'. These critics juxtapose unreality, error and subjectivity on the one side to realism, truth and objectivity on the other, insisting that we must somehow choose between them.

This is a challenging position; I will later argue that if socialism is to be viable, it must find a way of overcoming this dualism — so that it is both realist and utopian at the same time.

Bauman's views on utopia

Bauman, in a work revealingly entitled *Socialism as Utopia* (1976), argues that we should view utopias positively — as a necessary condition of historical change. This would make the utopian society realistic, and part of the historical process. Bauman insists that a utopia 'sets the stage for a genuinely realistic politics'. It extends the meaning of realism to encompass the full range of possible options. Utopias make conscious the major divisions of interest within society: the future is portrayed as a set of competing projects.

Bauman draws a distinction between *perfection* as a stable and immutable state and *perfectibility* that paves the way for utopia. The latter concept, he argues, stresses movement rather than end point, and 'sets no limits to development, refusing even to discuss its supposedly final frontiers'. The problem is, however, that perfection as a concept remains. To say that humans are 'perfectible' does imply that they cannot merely improve, but become perfect — like gods. In my view, perfection, whatever form it takes, is a theological concept that inevitably contrasts utopia and reality.

Bauman argues that utopias are little concerned with 'pragmatically conceived realism' and they do not seem logical and immediate steps from what is in existence at present. This surely implies that a utopian critique does not work through the present, but somehow stands outside it. This is the problem.

If socialism is desirable in the sense that it 'breaks the bonds of the existing order', are we not still stuck with the 'sad dualism' that seems to project socialism as an 'ought' rather than an 'is'? It is still unclear as to whether we can ever have a society that is socialist. Bauman argues that socialism is the counter-culture of capitalist society, and this appears to suggest that socialists are no more than critics of capitalism and that socialism cannot be an empirical reality, a society in its own right.

Many of those sympathetic to socialism and utopia take the same view. Goodwin and Taylor in *The Politics of Utopia* (1982), for example, speak of the fact that utopias 'transcend the ubiquitous, seemingly unassailable present'. 'They help us to escape from the existent. They involve an instant or imminent transition from the present system: a break with history.' But this argument reproduces rather than transcends the opposition between 'is' and 'ought'.

While Goodwin and Taylor defend utopianism in political theory as a 'dynamic force', they see it as haunted by the problem of the leap from theory to practice. It is one thing to argue that socialism, like all ideals, simplifies the complexities of the real world. But it is quite another to suggest that there is an unbridgeable gulf between ideal and reality, for this means that utopias are abstract in a pejorative sense: they are necessarily unrealistic, unhistorical, static, perfectionist etc.

Whether writers are sympathetic to socialism and utopianism or, like John Gray, opposed to both, the adoption of a traditional view of utopia means that socialism is still the abstract 'ought' at odds with the concrete 'is'. It is vulnerable to the argument that it stands outside the real world.

Conclusion

Socialism is a doctrine and a political movement that exists in a considerable number of different forms. However, although socialisms are extremely variegated, socialism in general can be defined as a movement that extols co-operation, is critical of capitalism, has a positive view of freedom and believes in some kind of equality.

Socialism is vulnerable to the criticism that it is utopian — that it subscribes to a belief in humanity and society that is unrealistic and at odds with our experience. Although socialism is a broad church, it excludes doctrines and movements that are hostile to the ideals of the Enlightenment (even though these movements might be regarded as 'socialistic' or have socialism in their title), since socialism subscribes to a notion of freedom and equality.

Summary

- Socialism exists in a wide variety of forms, but a major distinction can be made between Marxism and social democracy. The British Labour Party has for this reason always rejected attempts by the British Communist Party to affiliate. Marxists are also divided among themselves.
- All socialism involves an optimistic view of human nature, a belief in cooperation, a positive concept of freedom and an emphasis on the importance of equality.
- Socialism in general suffers from the problem of utopia. Commentators differ as to whether utopias are a good or a bad thing, and socialists for their part are uncertain as to whether utopias can be realised or are a mere desire that cannot be attained.

Task 1.1

Read the passage below and answer the questions that follow.

Was National Socialist Germany socialist?

Following the collapse of the German war effort a republic was created. An uprising of the left was smashed by a socialist government that cooperated with the army and the employers. Hitler, who had fought in the First World War, made contact with the German Workers' Party (DAP or Deutsche Arbeiterpartei). After being demobilised in 1920 he became leader of the DAP, which was then renamed the National Socialist German Workers' Party (NSDAP).

Adolf Hitler in 1944

Illustrated London News

The socialist identity of the party was continually stressed in the 1920s. Unemployment was extremely high: investment and industry collapsed, and the first programme of the party spoke of the need to share profits, nationalise the trusts, increase pensions and provide free education. Some Nazis like Strasser (1892–1934) attacked capitalism, while Goebbels (1897–1945) said in 1928 that 'no honest thinking person today would want to deny the justification of the workers' movements'. A body was set up to advance Nazi interests among the trade unions, and the programme of the party continued to advocate what was called 'soldierly socialism'.

Questions

1 Is socialism a sufficiently broad concept to incorporate Nazism?
2 Nazis drew support from the workers. Is this enough to make the Nazi movement socialist?
3 Is anti-capitalism evidence of a socialist programme?
4 Is socialism a militaristic doctrine?
5 'The Nazis were strongly opposed to liberalism.' Is this enough to make their movement socialist?

Guidance

In thinking about whether Nazism should be seen as a form of socialism, the following points should be borne in mind:
● Nazism was militantly nationalistic, whereas socialism builds upon the liberal idea that all humans must be liberated.

Task 1.1 (continued)

- Nazism was hostile to the notion of equality and the idea of democracy (however it was interpreted).
- Those Nazis who claimed to be socialists were liquidated in the 'Night of the Long Knives', when the leaders of the Stormtrooper movement (unemployed war veterans) were shot by the SS.
- Large industrialists were wooed for their support, and although many employers thought that Hitler was 'tactless' and considered his economic progress 'utopian', his militant anti-communism appealed to them and their support was crucial to his becoming chancellor in 1933.
- Support for the Nazis came particularly from those who believed themselves threatened with unemployment (rather than those who were actually unemployed) and they tended to be members of the lower middle class rather than industrial workers.
- The German economy remained capitalistic, although with extensive state control. There were some features of Nazism that employers disliked (e.g. the banning of women from the labour force) but in general they backed Nazi policies. Indeed, during the 1933 general election Jewish businessmen even contributed money to Hitler's party, even though after 1933 all Jews were subject to the most horrendous persecution.

Mary Evans

A parade of Stormtroopers at a Nuremberg Rally, *c.* 1938

Task 1.2

Using this chapter and other resources available to you, answer the following questions:

1 Do socialists have a fanciful view of human nature?
2 Can socialists be authoritarian as well as democratic?
3 Is it possible to be a socialist and reject the idea of equality?

4 Is socialism possible?

5 Does socialism have a plausible view of freedom?

Guidance

Question 1

Socialists believe that human nature can be changed. They are conscious of the fact that people in contemporary capitalist society display all kinds of behavioural traits that stand in the way of socialist ethics. People are greedy, self-interested, opportunistic and short-termist. Socialist ethics require them to be egalitarian, generous, cooperative and community-minded. Can people change, or is the socialist view of a transformed human nature simply a pipe dream?

There are two problems that socialists need to address. The first is the issue of authoritarianism. It is tempting to 'remould' people through state intervention, based on a view that people don't appreciate their real interests and must be told, and even forced, to change. This is a short cut that will certainly be counterproductive. People are influenced by their circumstances and the levels of insecurity, inequality and exploitation in a capitalist society make it inevitable that people will behave in 'unsocialist' ways. Socialists need patience if people are to see the error of their ways.

The second problem relates to the need for socialists to be realistic and practical. It is crucial to try to demonstrate that it is in people's self-interest to cooperate and respect others; that inequality generates problems that spare nobody. Even the rich suffer from crime and insecurity. Changing human nature is therefore not a question of preaching 'goodness' from the outside as it were, but showing people that they can be better consumers and attend to personal and family interests if they address themselves to long-term questions like the environment and peace. People have already changed — in the attitude towards gay people in the West, for example — and they can change further.

Question 2

It is sometimes argued that socialists cannot espouse the notion of freedom and equality unless they are also democratic. An 'undemocratic socialist' is, according to this argument, a contradiction in terms.

It is certainly true that socialism can be democratic. Socialists, particularly in the West, have embraced Parliament, elections and supported liberal values. Socialists therefore can be democratic, rejecting the need for revolution where liberal institutions exist, and urging toleration for their opponents.

But socialism can be authoritarian as well. Engels described revolution as the most authoritarian thing there is, and where socialists embrace revolution, then authoritarianism is likely to follow. Socialists can and have identified their opponents

Task 1.2 (continued)

as counter-revolutionaries who need to be crushed rather than tolerated, even when these opponents have sought to challenge socialism or a particular kind of socialism in peaceful and legal ways. The abuses of human rights associated with Stalin, Mao and Pol Pot, for example, do not mean that these regimes were not socialist. They sought egalitarian and cooperative ends, but in an oppressive and authoritarian manner.

Question 3

People have called themselves socialists while rejecting the notion of equality. The Nazis (or National Socialists) argued that Jews, gay people and travellers (to take just three groups of their victims) were inferior beings and a threat to the purity of the German nation. The notion of equality stems from liberalism and the European Enlightenment and right-wing extremists reject liberal values, regarding them as decadent and dangerous.

However, this is why the claim by the Nazis to be socialist should be resisted. It is impossible to be a socialist and openly and explicitly espouse racist and sexist notions. Socialism arose historically as a response to what was perceived to be the liberal failure to practise what was preached. Socialists interpret freedom and equality differently from liberals, but it is impossible to be a socialist and reject equality as an ideal. Of course, socialists may not respect equality in practice — special shops for Communist Party members in eastern Europe violated egalitarian norms. But all forms of socialism claim to be egalitarian, even if they interpret equality in controversial ways, and may even see equality as an end that can only be realised in the future.

Question 4

Critics of socialism argue that socialism is unworkable, that attempts to realise it create human misery and that it is a system that is contrary to human nature, and is therefore impossible. They point to the many failures of socialism. The collapse of the Communist Party states was seen by some liberals and most conservatives as evidence of 'the death of socialism' — that such a system is doomed to implode.

Socialists might reply in a number of ways, however. They might liken socialism to Gandhi's quip about Western civilisation — 'a good idea but it has never been tried'; that Stalinism, for example, is a caricature of what socialism could be like, and that trying to build socialism in 'backward' conditions leads to a backward form of socialism. Or they might argue that while authoritarian kinds of socialism are unworkable, this is not true of democratic socialism where the planning process is piecemeal and pragmatic, and institutions are established (like the National Health Service in the UK, for example) that already embrace socialist ethics. Socialism does not need to be conceived of as a revolutionary and complete alternative to capitalism: it can be conceived of as inroads into market practices so that people gradually

Task 1.2 (continued)

develop more sociable and cooperative ways of organising society. This kind of socialism is not only possible, but we can already point to evidence of its success.

Question 5

Socialists support what is usually called a positive notion of freedom. By this is meant a 'freedom to' — freedom as power. To give a typical example: freedom to read and write, when construed positively, means that a person can actually read and write so that material resources must be provided to make this possible.

This is a plausible view of freedom provided that it also incorporates a 'negative' view of freedom — 'freedom from' — freedom as the absence of deliberate interference. 'On its own' positive freedom is not plausible because having the power to read and write is hardly adequate if people can be punished for speaking their mind. Authoritarian societies might have high levels of literacy — and this is good — but if there is, say, fierce censorship, then positive freedom 'on its own' is not enough. It must be linked to negative freedom so that a person not only has the capacity to read and write, but the space to do so. Socialists must, in other words, respect negative freedoms (linked to the liberal tradition) and ensure that positive freedoms take these for granted. Just as it is not acceptable to argue that people have the right to speak and write freely when they lack the capacity to do, so having the capacity is inadequate if penalties are exacted against those who speak their mind or write in ways that displease the powers that be.

Useful websites

- www.spartacus.schoolnet.co.uk
- www.inter-change-search.net/directory/Society/Politics/Socialism/
- www.the-wood.org/socialism/

Further reading

- Bauman, Z. (1976) *Socialism as Utopia*, George Allen & Unwin.
- Crick, B. (1963) *In Defence of Politics*, 2nd edn, Penguin.
- Crick, B. (1987) *Socialism*, Open University Press.
- Geoghegan, V. (1987) *Utopianism and Marxism*, Methuen.
- Goodwin, B. and Taylor, K. (1982) *The Politics of Utopia*, Hutchinson.
- Heywood, A. (1992) *Political Ideologies*, Macmillan.
- Mannheim, K. (1936) *Ideology and Utopia*, Routledge.
- Wright, A. (1996) *Socialisms*, Routledge.

Is socialism utopian?

Friedrich Engels, Marx's friend and collaborator, wrote a fierce polemic against a German socialist by the name of Dühring and later published a work based upon his polemic entitled *Socialism: Utopian and Scientific*. In this work Engels characterised Marxism as a 'scientific' doctrine, and three socialists were singled out as being utopian. They were:

- Henri de Saint-Simon (1760–1825)
- Charles Fourier (1773–1837)
- Robert Owen (1771–1858)

In fact, each of them considered their own work to be scientific and practical.

Friedrich Engels

Introducing the (so-called) utopians

Saint-Simon

Saint-Simon took the view that the French Revolution had neglected class structure in the name of human rights. He included industrialists and bankers in the 'producing' class, believing that workers and capitalists have a unity of interests, sustained by what Saint-Simon believed would be a spread of wealth and ownership across society as a whole.

Is it right to call his argument 'utopian'? Saint-Simon believed that the old order had unwittingly produced the basis for a new order, and indeed, he sounds like a Marxist steeped in Hegelian dialectics when he argues that

Henri de Saint-Simon

'everything is relative — that is the only absolute'. His celebrated argument, that the state gives way to administration (so central to Marxist theory), was based upon a belief that the modern credit and banking system had already demonstrated its attachment to scientific principles, and that these could exert a discipline that would make the state redundant.

Why did Engels call this system 'utopian' when it so manifestly stresses the importance of science and historical necessity? Saint-Simon clearly does not fit into Engels's view that modern socialism is based upon the class antagonism between capitalist and wage-worker. But it does seem unfair to ascribe to Saint-Simon (as Engels does to the utopians in general) the view that socialism is not an 'inevitable event' but a happy accident, when Saint-Simon had laid so much emphasis on science and historical development.

Fourier

Fourier, on the other hand, did consider the workers and capitalists to have conflicting interests. He was particularly concerned at the way in which the Industrial Revolution has stripped work of its pleasure. His solution was to establish 'phalanteres' — cooperative communities of some 1,600 people working in areas of around 5,000 acres in the countryside or small towns. Fourier was adamant that his was not a utopian socialism.

Charles Fourier

He described utopias as 'dreams', schemes without an effective method that have 'led people to the very opposite of the state of well-being they promised them'. He believed that his socialism was based on a scientific project for reconstruction. Indeed, so precise a science was socialism that Fourier took the view that civilised society has 144 evils; humans have 12 basic passions; they do 12 different jobs; and they need 9 meals a day to sustain them.

Owen

Robert Owen saw himself as a practical, hard-headed person of business, and he owned cotton mills in New Lanark in Scotland. He was struck as to how, under rational socialist management, these mills could still be profitable, and he decided to advocate village cooperatives of between 300 and 2,000 people working land between 600 and 1,800 acres. It is true that his schemes were dogged by failure.

The community that he established at New Harmony in the USA collapsed after 3 years in 1827, and his labour bazaars, at which goods were to exchange according to the amount of labour embodied in them, did not survive the economic crisis of 1834. His national trade union was called a 'grand national moral union for the productive classes', but his dictatorial leadership demonstrated the problem with his theory of character. Character was, in Owen's view, externally determined, so that only an exceptional person (like Owen!) could initiate reform for a relatively passive population.

Robert Owen

He did, however, have a lasting effect on the British labour movement as a practical reformer, and the consumer cooperatives that he advocated — the Co-op stores — still exist on high streets in British cities today. Although Owen's notion of science stemmed from an uncritical reading of the Enlightenment, he certainly regarded himself as a person of scientific, secular and empirical values. Indeed, a youthful Engels was to describe Owen's views as 'the most practical and fully worked out' of all the socialists.

Marxism and utopianism

Marx (1818–83) and Engels (1820–95) adopted a traditional view of utopia. What makes Saint-Simon a utopian, in my opinion, is not that his views are problematic, but merely that he poses a radical alternative to feudal rather than bourgeois society. One could argue that his utopianism is contentious, given the fact that he ignores the conflicts of interest between workers and capitalists. But this is because he is a *poor* or flawed utopian, not because he is a utopian per se.

The same is true of the other two socialists who are regarded as utopians by Marx and Engels. Indeed, Engels in his youth referred to Fourier's 'scientific research, cool, unbiased systematic thought'. The point here is that

Illustrated London News
Karl Marx

Fourier's ideas, stimulating as they are, are unworkable, and Owen's village communities are naïve and his theory of character one-sided.

Marx and Engels's critique of the three 'utopians' is basically sensible, but what is problematic is the idea that they are utopians whereas Marx and Engels are not. People like Saint-Simon, Fourier and Owen ignored the need for a political struggle to achieve their objectives; they overlooked the conflicts of interest involved in posing a socialist solution, the need for allies, the importance of designating stages, and the fact that a resort to violence is justifiable under certain conditions. But these arguments make them unrealistic utopians, not utopians per se.

There is some ambivalence in the literature as to whether Marx and Engels were utopians. Heywood (as noted above) describes communism as 'a utopian vision of a future society envisaged and described by Marx and Engels'. On the other hand, he argues that Marx and Engels supported 'scientific socialism' and rejected what they called 'utopian socialism'. It is worth noting how strongly influenced Marx and Engels were by the 'utopian' socialists, and 'utopian' notions of 'harmony', 'association', 'community' and 'cooperation' appear in their own work.

Marx, Engels and socialism

The belief that socialism should be scientific and not utopian is, therefore, highly contentious. There is also a terminological point that we need to tackle right away. In the *Communist Manifesto* of 1848 Engels argued that the term 'communism' was preferred because it was seen as a working-class movement from below. Socialism, on the other hand, was a respectable movement initiated from above. However, later Marxists called themselves socialists and social democrats. It was only after 1917, when Lenin and the Bolsheviks wanted to distance themselves from other socialists (who had supported the First World War and opposed the Russian Revolution), that the term 'Communist' was resurrected.

Berki has argued in his book *Socialism* (1975) that Marx transformed socialism from underdog to a 'fully grown part of the modern landscape'. Both Marx and Engels prized scholarship and learning highly. Marx was a philosopher, who devoted most of his life to studying political economy, and in 1867 he published *Das Kapital*, or *Capital*, a work that Engels was to describe as the bible of the working class. Engels, for his part, read and wrote widely about natural science, anthropology, history, politics and economics, and both Marx and Engels regarded science not as the pursuit of facts rather than values but simply as coherent and systematic thought.

Why did Engels in particular see Saint-Simon, Fourier and Owen as utopians? In the *Communist Manifesto* Marx and Engels praised the 'utopians' for producing 'the most valuable materials for the enlightenment of the working class'. Measures like the abolition of the distinction between town and country; the disappearance of the family; the wages system; the private ownership of industry; the dying out of the state; and a positive relationship between the individual and society were suggested by the 'utopians' and became part of Marx and Engels's own arguments. Nevertheless, the label is contentious, for Marx and Engels clearly regarded the 'utopians' as painting 'fantastic pictures of a future society', a fantasy that reflected the historically undeveloped state of the working class itself.

Marxism as a 'scientific socialism'

Why was Marxism seen as scientific? Marxism, Marx and Engels argued, is a scientific socialism because it is:

- **a theory of class conflict.** It holds that in class-divided societies there are incompatible social interests that lead to exploitation. This is why class is both an economic and a political reality, since between the classes there is war. In contrast, the utopians seek change through general principles of 'reason' and 'justice'.
- **a theory of revolution.** Such is the incompatibility of class interests that change can only come through revolution. Although the *Communist Manifesto* describes revolution in violent terms, Marx's later position was that revolutions can be peaceful, even constitutional, but they will be violent if necessary. Because classes are political as well as economic entities, they seek to control the state in their own interest, so that the state has a class character. Utopians, by contrast, seek peaceful and sometimes piecemeal change, appealing to all classes in society for support, and invariably see the state as part of the solution rather than part of the problem.
- **a theory of history.** All societies are basically moulded by the conflict between the forces of production (which embrace science and technology) and the relations of production (the system of ownership). These two elements form a basis upon which arises a 'superstructure' that incorporates political institutions, educational systems, culture and ideas. In class-divided societies the conflict between the forces and relations of production creates the need for revolution, so that under capitalism the social character of the forces of production comes into sharp and increasing conflict with the private relations of production. That is why revolution is inevitable. After this revolution class

divisions disappear, and with the disappearance of these divisions the need for a state itself 'withers'.

- **a theory of society.** Central to this theory of history is a theory of society that argues that people enter into relations of production 'independent of their will'. This means that although human activity is a conscious activity, the consequences of this activity are never the same as those intended. Capitalism is seen as a system that unwittingly creates the working class, educates them through factory production, goads them into struggle and ultimately drives them to revolution. By way of contrast, 'utopians' do not see capitalism as a contradictory system, a system that is self-destructive. They do not accept the particular role of the workers in providing leadership to a political movement for social emancipation, nor do they accept the need for a Communist or socialist party to provide leadership for revolution. Socialism, as far as they see it, is merely 'desirable' and not inevitable.

Conclusion

Marx and Engels presented their socialism as 'scientific' and characterised the socialism of their rivals as 'utopian'. Not only is this view unfair, since all three 'classic utopians' — Saint-Simon, Fourier and Owen — regarded themselves as scientific, but it could well be argued that Marx and Engels's socialism is utopian as well. Indeed, when the theory of Marxism is presented it is clear that Marx and Engels owed a good deal to the thinkers that they rather scornfully dismissed.

Summary

- Nineteenth-century socialists like Saint-Simon, Fourier and Owen were seen by Marx and Engels as utopians, although it is noteworthy that the latter did not see themselves in these terms.
- It could be argued that Marx and Engels were also utopians, since their own vision of socialism did not exist in reality.
- Marx and Engels preferred the term 'Communist' in the *Communist Manifesto* but generally used the terms 'socialism' and 'communism' indifferently. It was only after the Russian Revolution that the term 'socialism' became identified with what we would call today 'social democracy'.
- Marx and Engels claimed that their theory of socialism was scientific because it was rooted in class divisions and class conflict and involved a theory of society and history that centred on the clash between the forces and relations of production.

Task 2.1

Read the passage below and answer the question that follows.

William Morris — a Marxist utopia?

William Morris's *News from Nowhere* is set in England about 100 years after capitalism has been overthrown through violent revolution. The central figure goes to bed in winter and awakes in mid-summer, and takes a walk along the Thames. The boatman who takes him up the river is astonished and puzzled by the money that is offered. The visitor is taken through Hammersmith — now with pleasant country lanes and fields. The buildings are exquisite, the women beautiful, and poverty vanquished. He travels to Kensington and passes onto Piccadilly.

He is treated with great generosity in shops that no longer take money. In Trafalgar Square he notes the elegant and ornamented houses. There is no formal education, the Houses of Parliament are used to store dung, and prisons do not exist. Work is enjoyable. The central figure visits an old man who has a house near the British Museum, who tells him that courts of law have disappeared and the country overall has become a garden full of beautiful and tasteful dwellings. There is no state and there are no criminals, with majorities deciding matters of common interest. The country is living under a tolerant and agreeable communism. There are markets but they are institutions through which people obtain what they need.

Those who act antisocially are simply 'punished' by the remorse they feel. The guest (as he is called) returns to Hammersmith and is taken by boat up the Thames, stopping at Hampton Court for a meal and continuing on to Runnymede, where he is told about the revolution and civil war. He then travels to Oxford, and the dream (or vision as Morris prefers to call it) ends.

This work not only acknowledges the existence of non-violent conflict, but also allows for the occasional murder. The use of social sanctions in *News from Nowhere* to handle serious ethical infringements is interesting and challenging. It is clear that the past has left its mark on the Communist society, since there are still a few eccentrics who hanker after the capitalist society of old.

Women are treated in a mildly sexist manner — they still manage the house and wait on men, and Levitas in *The Concept of Utopia* (1990) is surely right to say that Morris continues to support the sexual division of labour. But centrally problematic to his whole portrait is that he aggravates the static implications of the classical Marxist view of communism by identifying it as 'an epoch of rest' (the subtitle of the book — which Morton omits from his edition of *News from Nowhere*) and he sees communism as a society of 'fulfilled aspirations', 'vision of all my longings for rest and peace'. As Thompson comments in his classic *William Morris: Romantic to Revolutionary* (1977), 'Unceasing criticism, boundless curiosity in the ways and

Task 2.1 (continued)

thoughts' of the past has gone. In *News from Nowhere* the narrator is told: 'We have been living for a hundred and fifty years at least, more or less in our present manner.'

Thompson points out that Morris doubted that 'bourgeois' individualism had made any real contribution to human consciousness and his reference to the great artists of the past 400 years was without any warmth. Morris disliked Puritanism so intensely that he could not bring himself to read Milton. Indeed, Perry Anderson takes the view in his *Arguments in English Marxism* (1980) that Morris repressed and rejected (rather than built upon) the history of capitalism. Kinna, in her *William Morris: The Art of Socialism* (2000), argues that *News from Nowhere* drew upon a 'well-developed model of medieval England'. Morris assumes that the new architecture is necessarily gothic in character.

Morris's *News from Nowhere* is problematic, not because it is utopian, but because it has static and ahistorical features that make it implausible as a portrait of the future. 'This is not the age of inventions', says one of the characters. Morris speaks of having moved 'into the present rest and happiness of complete Communism'. Morris is an important figure in this discussion because he is regarded by Geoghegan as the 'first self-consciously utopian Marxist'. Does he succeed in bridging the gulf between science and utopia that is central to the classical Marxist position? A. L. Morton, in *The English Utopia* (1952), says of Morris's *News from Nowhere* that 'it is the first Utopia which is not utopian', and Thompson in his work on Morris refers to *News from Nowhere* as 'a Scientific Utopia', a work in which the world of dream and the world of reality are reunited. Kinna comments that for Morris, 'as an imaginary ideal, utopia can be compared to the idea of paradise'. Morris had written an essay dealing with 'the Promised Land of Socialism', although he saw his utopia as a realisable goal.

Thompson's argument is that *News from Nowhere* might be scientific, 'And yet it is still is a Utopia, which only a writer nurtured in the romantic tradition could have conceived.' In his Postscript, Thompson argues that Engels's rather disdainful view of Morris (he saw Morris as a 'sentimental socialist') reflects a tendency by Marx and Engels to dismiss Romanticism as 'moralism' and 'utopianism'. The French critic Abensour argues that Morris espouses a new utopianism: he is concerned with the liberation of desire — to desire in a different way, not with the static, perfectionist models of traditional utopias. It is certainly true that *News from Nowhere* breaks from the traditionalist concept of utopia in significant ways.

Question

In the following pairs of statements, which of the two views would you support?

1 (a) Morris's *News from Nowhere* is an inspiring work.

   (b) Morris's *News from Nowhere* is just a rather silly fantasy.

Task 2.1 (continued)

2 (a) Morris makes a socialist society much more meaningful by showing how it actually works.

(b) Morris simply projects his romantic nostalgia onto the future in an indulgent and implausible way.

3 (a) Marx and Engels were right to ridicule attempts by socialists to construct utopias.

(b) Marx and Engels were just as utopian as those whom they ridiculed.

4 (a) Socialism requires some sentiment and romanticism.

(b) Socialism is ridiculous unless it bases its principles on hard-headed facts.

Task 2.2

Using this chapter and other resources available to you, answer the following questions:

1 Do you agree with the view that the doctrines of Saint-Simon, Fourier and Owen were utopian in character?

2 Why did Marx and Engels object to what they called 'utopianism'?

3 Why does Marxism claim to be a science?

4 Is 'scientific socialism' a contradiction in terms?

5 'Marx and Engels were more indebted to the "utopians" than many realise.' Discuss.

Guidance

Question 1

It is certainly true that the views of Saint-Simon, Fourier and Owen can be criticised. Saint-Simon, after all, believed that whereas the landed gentry were parasitic, capitalists were not. What about those who make money through speculation? Is this work? Fourier spoke of the need to establish communities composed of a particular number of people: does this not tie our hands in a world of shifting populations and ever-changing methods of production? Owen wanted groups to manage their own lives, and yet he saw himself as a benevolent reformer who would bring enlightenment to passive and suffering souls.

Each of these socialists had their deficiencies, but although they disliked the term, they can be called utopian because they posed alternatives to existing society. But the term 'utopian' is often a negative one that implies fantasy or unreality. It is true that the three socialists had unworkable schemes, but this is because they put forward bad utopias, not because they were utopian per se.

Question 2

Marx and Engels were correct to criticise other socialists. They warned that socialism cannot be achieved merely because it seems like a good idea. People must experience

Task 2.2 (continued)

problems with the market and capitalism for themselves, forge alliances with other like-minded people and campaign for change. We can certainly challenge the argument that socialism can be brought about by a benevolent reformer, or that it is simply an appealing idea, or that it does not require particular conditions to make it relevant.

Marx and Engels sought to address these deficiencies with their own version of socialism, arguing that other socialists had a purely negative view of capitalism and a belief that principles of justice and equality were eternal. But their own view of socialism has its problems. A belief that revolution was the inevitable outcome of class struggle led to elitism and authoritarianism, and an attack on static principles was accompanied by an apparent disdain for moral ideas of any kind.

Question 3

Marx and Engels claimed to be 'scientific' because they sought to base their theories on historical realities. This meant that socialism could not be realised at any time in the past or simply because a person had a strong desire to bring about a socialist world. Socialism, they argued, had to build upon capitalism and without capitalism, 'scientific' socialism was impossible. Capitalist society was seen as demolishing the repressive hierarchies of the feudal and absolutist past and, through the Industrial Revolution, creating a modern working class. Ironically, capitalism is the 'teacher' of the proletarian — the people without property — so that it is through the experience that workers have of factory life that workers learn the need for trade unions and a political party to advance their interests.

The division of society into classes with irreconcilable interests was deemed inevitable and although capitalism had initially served humanity by destroying feudalism, it became increasingly self-destructive as speculation, overproduction and unemployment took root. Socialism is not seen simply as desirable: it will happen whether we like it or not. It is the product of historical realities that scientific-minded revolutionaries must recognise. It is true that the role of Communists is to provide active leadership, but they will only succeed if their policies are based upon a sober respect for social trends and practical developments.

Question 4

There are two arguments against the notion of 'scientific socialism'. One is weak and one is strong. The weak argument contends that no 'ism' can be a science, and because socialism advocates a particular way of ordering society it cannot be scientific. This is a weak argument since it assumes that ideologies violate science, whereas the truth is that ideologies can be scientific where their postulates are factually based and correspond to historical realities.

What makes the notion of 'scientific socialism' as defined by Marx and Engels contestable is the idea that science is necessarily opposed to utopia. But if we define

Task 2.2 (continued)

utopia simply as an alternative to the present order, then a utopian position can be scientific if it is based upon a realistic appraisal of the world around us. Marx's theory is therefore also utopian, and to the extent that it approximates to the real world it can be called scientific as well. The strong argument, therefore, challenges the idea that if socialism is scientific, it cannot be utopian.

Question 5

Marx and Engels were certainly scathing about those whom they called 'utopian'. They accused them of ignoring the importance of class, revolution, political organisa- tion, and the need to base socialism upon the historical development of capitalism.

But not only can Marx and Engels's own theory be described as utopian as well, but many of their ideas came from the 'utopian' thinkers:

- the idea that socialism is a community
- the notion that socialism must tackle the problem of the division of labour in the factory, and the division between town and country in society at large
- the idea that socialists must support the emancipation of women and the democra- tisation of the family
- the argument that organised religion can encourage people to seek solutions in heaven rather than on earth
- the notion that a socialist society must be stateless as well as classless in character

Useful websites

- www.marxist.org.uk/htm_docs/princip2.htm
- www.socialistparty.org.uk/manifesto/m2frame.htm?manifesto.html
- www.spartacus.schoolnet.co.uk

Further reading

- Anderson, P. (1980) *Arguments within English Marxism*, Verso.
- Berki, R. N. (1975) *Socialism*, Dent.
- Engels, F. (1880) *Socialism: Utopian and Scientific*, in *Marx/Engels Selected Works*, Progress, 1968.
- Kinna, R. E. (2000) *William Morris: The Art of Socialism*, University of Wales Press.
- Levitas, R. (1990) *The Concept of Utopia*, Syracuse University Press.
- Morton, A. L. (1952) *The English Utopia*, Lawrence & Wishart.
- Thompson, E. P. (1977) *William Morris: Romantic to Revolutionary*, Merlin Press.

Can Marxism be a socialism that is democratic?

There are a number of problems with the theory (and not merely the practice) of 'scientific socialism'. They can be listed as:

- the argument of inevitability (the major problem)
- the theory of class war
- a rejection of 'moralism'
- the question of leadership (a relatively minor problem)

It will be argued that together these problems explain why Communist Party states following the theory of 'scientific socialism' have proved vulnerable to popular (even proletarian) protest.

Attempts to make Communist Party states more democratic were resisted by the Soviet leadership in 1968 and today only North Korea, Cuba, China and Vietnam remain as Communist Party states. Former Communist Party states changed their names — usually to include 'democracy' in their title — and they invariably describe themselves as socialist rather than Communist. What relationship exists between the hapless fate of these states and the theory of scientific socialism? It is worth giving this question some thought.

Introducing the inevitability argument

In Part I of the *Communist Manifesto* the victory of the proletariat is described as 'inevitable', as in the famous comment that 'what the bourgeoisie…produces, above all, is its own grave-diggers. Its fall and the victory of the proletariat are equally inevitable.' This has become a central theme of Marxism in general, and Engels was to argue that revolutions are 'the necessary outcome of circumstances, quite independent of the will or guide of particular parties'.

Marxism claims to be 'scientific' because it arises from the real movement of history that compels people to do things whether they like it or not. Revolution is (in some sense of the term) a 'natural' process, driven by the antagonistic conflict between the forces and relations of production at the heart of society. It is therefore unavoidable. There are a number of problems with the 'inevitability argument'.

What happens when revolutions are 'bourgeois' in character?

In the *Communist Manifesto* Marx and Engels declare that 'Communists everywhere support every revolutionary movement against the existing order of things'. Contrary to the 'utopians' who support socialism rather than capitalism, Marxists will support a 'bourgeois revolution' in countries where liberal constitutionalism has yet to prevail: in Germany, as the *Communist Manifesto* points out, Communists will fight with the bourgeoisie where the latter are acting in a revolutionary way. This notion is of the utmost importance as it explains the attraction of Marxism in colonial countries or autocratic regimes of a feudal or semi-feudal kind. But what has a liberal revolution to do with communism?

One of the most contentious aspects of the *Communist Manifesto* derives from the argument that once the old absolutist regime has fallen, 'the fight against the bourgeoisie itself may immediately begin'. The argument here focuses on Germany in 1848. Given the much more advanced conditions of European civilisation and 'a much more developed proletariat', 'the bourgeois revolution in Germany will be but the prelude to an immediately following proletarian revolution'.

Troops charging the crowds in Berlin during the revolution of 1848

This sentence was seen by the Bolsheviks as giving the October Revolution its classical Marxist credentials, since the Russia of 1917 was deemed analogous to the Germany of 1848, because of the combination of material backwardness and heightened political consciousness. The destruction of tsarism — the bourgeois revolution — could then be 'the prelude to an immediately following proletarian revolution'.

Hunt's arguments

Hunt has argued at some length in *The Political Ideas of Marx and Engels* (1974) that reference to 'the prelude to an immediately following proletarian revolution' — a formulation that occurs nowhere else in Marx's writing — was put in to appease the members of the Communist League who commissioned the *Manifesto*. They did not like the idea of a bourgeois revolution anyway, but a bourgeois revolution immediately followed by a proletarian one was enough to sugar the pill.

Hunt's argument is that this notion of permanent revolution — that a bourgeois revolution becomes a proletarian one relatively quickly — does not square with classical Marxism and the emphasis placed elsewhere in the *Communist Manifesto* on the gradual, step-by-step education of the proletariat preparing them for revolution and power. Whatever tactical considerations played their part in this fateful formulation, the argument is never actually repudiated by Marx and Engels, although they did later speak of the *Communist Manifesto* as a 'historical document which we have no longer any right to alter'. Whether we find Hunt's argument convincing, the point is that the notion that one revolution can immediately follow another has had significant historical consequences, and has come to be seen as part and parcel of Marxist theory.

The historical significance of the permanent revolution thesis

In 1967, 100 years had elapsed since the publication of Marx's *Das Kapital*. It was noted that were Marx to look around the world, he would be gratified as to how influential his views had become, but puzzled at the fact that this influence was concentrated in relatively 'backward' countries. In the countries where he might have expected his theories to prevail — the advanced industrialised societies of western Europe — his work was generally distrusted.

There can be little doubt that what has made Marxism significant for movements in the so-called Third World is the argument that relatively undeveloped countries can become socialist or Communist without the lengthy period of preparation that capitalism unwittingly and normally allows the proletariat.

Since this period is precisely the one in which workers become familiar with liberal ideas and institutions, it is not difficult to see that the omission or dramatic compression of such a period can only increase the need for the authoritarian leadership of a 'vanguard' party, and authoritarian political institutions themselves. Is it surprising then that the USSR, and later the People's Republic of China, followed a development in which the liberal tradition was suppressed rather than made the basis for further political advance?

The problem of 'premature' revolutions

Engels told the German socialist Weydemeyer that 'we shall find ourselves compelled to make Communist experiments and leaps which no one knows better than ourselves to be untimely'. But if revolution is deemed inevitable, then Marxists will 'find themselves' compelled to support 'experiments' and 'leaps' which are not only untimely, but can only be sustained by authoritarian institutions.

A good example of this problem can be seen in relation to Marx and Engels's attitude towards the Paris Commune (see Box 3.1). Because of the heroism of the Communards, Marx extolled the virtues of the commune. This he did in a book called *The Civil War in France* (1871), which outlined a radical polity that became the basis of Lenin's blueprint in *The State and Revolution*, written in 1918.

Yet the commune was in reality influenced by Blanquism (a rather elitist and coercive egalitarianism named after the French socialist Blanqui, 1805–81) and anarchist trends, and reflected what has been called 'an unsophisticated anti-bureaucratism' — an anti-bureaucratism that enshrined anti-liberal political practices.

Despite his private reservations, Marx felt obliged publicly to support an 'experiment' that could only have succeeded if power had been concentrated in an unambiguously authoritarian manner. Indeed, Marx described the formation of the Paris Commune in one of his letters as an act of 'desperate folly' and said that its leadership was 'in no wise socialist nor could it be'. Indeed, it is revealing that the commune scarcely received a mention at the Hague Conference of the First International a year later.

Box 3.1
The Paris Commune

The Paris Commune was created in 1871 after France was defeated by Prussia in the Franco-Prussian War. The French government tried to send in troops to prevent the Parisian National Guard's cannon from falling into the hands of the population. The soldiers refused to fire on the jeering crowd and turned their weapons on their officers.

In the elections called by the Parisian National Guard, the citizens of Paris elected a council made up of a majority of Jacobins and Republicans and a minority of socialists (mostly Blanquists — explicitly authoritarian socialists — and alongside them, followers of the anarchist Proudhon). This council proclaimed Paris autonomous and desired to recreate France as a confederation of communes (i.e. communities). Within the commune, the elected council people were paid an average wage. In addition, they had to report back to the people who had elected them and were subject to recall by electors if they did not carry out their mandates.

The Paris Commune began the process of creating a new society, one organised from the bottom up. By May, 43 workplaces were cooperatively run and the Louvre Museum became a munitions factory run by a workers' council. A meeting of the Mechanics' Union and the Association of Metal Workers argued that 'equality must not be an empty word' in the commune. The commune declared that the political unity of society was based on 'the voluntary association of all local initiatives, the free and spontaneous concourse of all individual energies for the common aim, the well-being, the liberty and the security of all'.

On 21 May government troops entered the city, and this was followed by 7 days of bitter street fighting. Squads of soldiers and armed members of the 'bourgeoisie' roamed the streets, killing and maiming at will. Over 25,000 people were killed in the street fighting, many murdered after they had surrendered, and their bodies were dumped in mass graves.

The commune lasted for 72 days and Marx, as president of the International Working Men's Association — the First International — expressed solidarity and support for the action. Yet 10 years later Marx declared that the commune was the rising of a city under exceptional conditions; that its majority was by no means socialist, nor could it be, and that with a 'modicum of common sense' a compromise with the French government at Versailles could have been reached.

Rosa Luxemburg, the Bolshevik Revolution and Stalinism

Marx's 'support' for the Paris Commune is not an isolated example. The Polish Marxist Rosa Luxemburg (1871–1919) was to defend the Bolshevik Revolution in the same way, and for the same reasons, that Marx and Engels had praised the Paris Commune. The Bolsheviks, she argued, have acted with immense heroism: the revolution was an act of proletarian courage, and she supported it.

Rosa Luxemburg giving a speech to a socialist gathering in Stuttgart, Germany

On the other hand, Luxemburg was alarmed by the authoritarianism of Lenin and Trotsky and she was particularly critical when the two leaders dispersed the Constituent Assembly in 1918 when it was returned with a socialist, but not a Bolshevik, majority. She thought that the revolution was bound to fail. In fact, the Russian Revolution succeeded by crushing its opponents, and Luxemburg, who was assassinated by German soldiers in 1919, never lived to see how a virtue was made of necessity first by Lenin and then by Stalin (Lenin resorted to terror; Stalin added to this a strategy of forced industrialisation — essential, he argued, if the threat from Nazi Germany was to be met).

A whole generation of Communists in liberal countries was prepared to support Stalin and Stalinism on the grounds that such rule was 'inevitable'. This position also created a grave dilemma for Stalin's critics like Trotsky, who supported the Russian Revolution and had shown his own illiberal tendencies. In his book on *Socialism* (1987), Crick expresses quite a common view when he says that 'it would have made little difference had Trotsky, not Stalin succeeded Lenin'. Indeed, Lesek Kolakowski, in his monumental *Main Current of Marxism*, comments that 'Stalin was Trotsky in actu' — the point is that both Stalin and Trotsky were Bolsheviks who made a virtue out of necessity, and both expressed a withering contempt for 'bourgeois democracy' and the liberal tradition.

Engels was to argue (in response to the anarchists) that 'revolution is the most authoritarian thing there is'. A theory that regards such an event as 'inevitable' will produce despotic political practices.

The concept of class war

Let us look at the other factors that arguably demonstrate a link between Marxism as a scientific socialism and the authoritarianism that created the popular upheavals in 1989. Marxism embraces a polarising concept of class war, and this can only reinforce its authoritarian consequences.

Such a concept has excluded or marginalised a whole series of struggles — for women's equality, gay rights, religious toleration, ecological sensitivity etc. — which are clearly central to the goal of emancipation, but which do not fit in with the notion that the proletariat and only the proletariat has a leading role to play.

Unrest in Bucharest, Romania, 1989

The problem of morality

In 1920 Ignazio Silone attended the Third Communist International (Comintern), which Lenin had set up. He recalled a discussion around the ultimatum that had been issued by the British Trades Union Congress (TUC), ordering its local branches not to support the minority movement — a movement that sought to build a rank-and-file organisation of trade unions — since the latter was led by the British Communist Party. A delegate from the British Communist Party explained the problems that this ultimatum had caused, only to be told by the Russian delegate that the local trade union branches should pretend to submit to the TUC while doing the opposite.

The British Communist interjected: 'But that would be a lie.' As Silone recalls:

> Loud laughter greeted this ingenuous objection, frank, cordial, interminable laughter, the like of which the gloomy offices of the Communist International had perhaps never heard before. The joke quickly spread over Moscow, for the Englishman's incredible and entertaining reply was telephoned at once to Stalin and to the most important offices of state, provoking new waves of mirth everywhere.

It is certainly true that Lenin and Stalin emphasised the weaknesses rather than the strengths of the Marxist tradition, but it can be argued that a disdain for moral argument lies in Marx's own writing.

Ends and means

Committed to the need for revolution as 'the most authoritarian thing there is', Marx and Engels tended to identify morality with the eternal principles of their 'utopian' rivals. It is true that they regarded exploitation as morally abominable, but the emphasis upon inevitability and historical necessity makes it relatively easy to see human rights as a luxury that no hard-headed revolutionary can afford.

Certainly the Russian Revolution encouraged the view that in a life-and-death struggle victory goes to the most efficient, not the most moral. Trotsky defended the need for terror against the enemies of Bolshevism with the rather chilling words: 'Who aims at the end cannot reject the means.' A dictatorship of the proletariat must use every conceivable method to protect itself.

Indeed, after the Moscow trials of 1936, in which a number of old Bolsheviks were executed on trumped-up charges, Trotsky could still argue that 'lying and deceit' are justifiable in class and civil war. As he put it, lying and worse 'are an inseparable part of the class struggle, even in its elementary forms'. At best we must choose between proletarian morality and bourgeois morality, so that there seems to be no place for human rights at all.

The question of leadership

Leadership is a problem for all political movements that seek to change society in the interests of the poor and the inarticulate, since people from relatively comfortable backgrounds will tend to monopolise leadership skills.

This is a general problem for all who want to change the world so as to further the interests of the 'people'. But the problem is aggravated by a belief that utopian ideals are mere fantasies. A 'scientific' attitude ought to be tolerant and empirical, but in Marxism, the notion of leaders spearheading revolutionary processes that are deemed inevitable and historically necessary, must give a further twist to an authoritarian version of socialism, whose state and political institutions are illiberal and — despite Marxist theory on this point — refuse to 'wither away'.

Conclusion

It can be argued that the so-called 'scientific' features of Marxism help to explain not why it is a superior kind of socialism, but why it is authoritarian in its theory and practice. The key feature here is the claim that socialism is inevitable — an argument that is linked to the problem of supporting non-socialist revolutions and revolutions that are 'premature'.

Indeed, Rosa Luxemburg supported the Russian Revolution with the same misgiving that Marx had extolled the Paris Commune. The belief in inevitability commits Marxists to identifying with historical events that may trample upon democratic values and principles. The doctrine of class struggle can also be problematic, and a disdainful attitude towards morality may lead to human rights abuses. All these aggravate the problem of a leadership that is both unrepresentative of, and unsympathetic to, the popular masses.

Summary

- Marxism as a scientific socialism tends to authoritarianism. The major cause of this is the belief that historical events are inevitable.
- This problem is aggravated by the argument that Communists must support all revolutions even when they are 'bourgeois', that is, they are concerned to bring about middle-class rather than socialist ends.

- Also problematic is the fact that revolutions might be premature, i.e. take place when material conditions do not justify them. Marx's public praise for the Paris Commune needs to be placed alongside his private view that its formation was foolish and bound to fail, while Luxemburg's attitude towards the Russian Revolution exemplifies the difficulties that the Marxist theory of revolution generates.
- A belief in the necessity of class war leads to polarisation and a disdain for morality. Morality is identified with weakness and sentimentality: to defend itself, a revolution must be prepared to murder, lie and deceive.
- Leadership is a general problem of all movements seeking popular emancipation, but it is a problem that a belief in scientific socialism, historical inevitability and class war can only aggravate.

Task 3.1

Read the passage below and answer the question that follows.

The Communist Party of Great Britain and the British Labour Party

In 1920 the International Communist Movement (the Comintern) instructed the Communist Party of Britain to seek affiliation with the Labour Party. The Labour Party was a federal body that had, in addition to trade unions, many political organisations like the Cooperative Party affiliated with it. The instruction from the Comintern caused some dismay among Communist Party members, but it was followed.

In his work *Left-wing Communism: An Infantile Disorder* (1920) Lenin had argued for affiliation; Tommy Jackson, one of the party's theoreticians, summarised Lenin's arguments, saying of the Labour Party leaders: 'I would take them by the hand as a preliminary to taking them by the throat.' In the 1922 election one of the Communists who stood as a Labour candidate was elected, while the other stood as a Communist but without Labour opposition.

In 1921 the Labour leaders had already rejected the request for affiliation on the grounds that the differences between the parties were 'insuperable'. After the Labour Party issued a questionnaire to the Communist Party, the executive's refusal to affiliate was upheld by a substantial majority at the Labour conference of 1922. In 1924 the Labour Party took the view that individual members of the Communist Party were not eligible to stand as Labour candidates. At the 1922 conference Frank Hodges of the Labour Party had described Communist Party members as 'intellectual slaves of Moscow...taking orders from the Asiatic mind'.

In 1927, 23 local Labour parties were disaffiliated because they continued to support the Communist-organised National Left Movement. In 1935 the Communist Party withdrew all but two candidates from the election, but these two faced an

Task 3.1 (continued)

official Labour opposition: again the Communist Party applied for affiliation and again this was rejected. In 1937 the Labour Party executive disaffiliated the Socialist League, which had entered into discussion with the Communist Party, and 2 years later those Labour Party members advocating a popular front with the Communists were expelled. In 1943 the Comintern was dissolved but this did not affect the decision of the Labour Party to reject affiliation once again. The issue was never raised officially after this.

Question

Imagine that you have been asked to judge an application by the Communist Party of Great Britain to affiliate to the Labour Party. Which of the arguments would weigh most strongly with you?

1 On the one hand...

The Labour Party has always espoused parliamentary democracy and constitutional change. It prefers Robert Owen to Karl Marx, and is suspicious of the doctrine of class war and revolution.

On the other hand...

The Communists are not seeking to 'take over' the party. They merely seek to become one of the constituent groups that make up the party. If the Cooperative Party can affiliate, why can't the Communists? It is not necessary to agree with Marxism any more than one has to go along with, say, the tenets of the Fabian Society — a group that is also affiliated with the Labour Party.

2 On the one hand...

The Communists belong to the Third International based in Moscow. It is clear that they are not an authentically British movement, and would propagate the interests of a foreign power if permitted to affiliate.

On the other hand...

There is an important precedent in the way that Eduard Bernstein, who came to Britain as a German Marxist, was converted to believing in a much more liberal form of socialism. Might the same happen to the Communists as well? Debating with members of the Labour Party could serve to help them see that a less authoritarian form of socialism is possible and desirable.

3 On the one hand...

Allowing Communists to affiliate to Labour would be a propaganda gift to the Conservatives in particular (and also to some Liberals). Labour's opponents could argue that socialism was itself a foreign doctrine serving the needs of a foreign power.

Task 3.1 (continued)

On the other hand...
The opponents of socialism will always try to discredit the Labour Party, whatever
it does. The affiliation of the Communists would encourage other members of the
Labour Party to spend more time thinking about wider philosophical questions, and
these members would be able to demonstrate the strength of democratic
socialism through directly engaging with Marxists with their different ideas.

Task 3.2

Using this chapter and other resources available to you, answer the following
questions:

1 Do you agree with the argument that a belief in historical inevitability has
authoritarian consequences for Marxism?
2 Are the views of Marx to 'blame' for the authoritarianism of Communist
Party states?
3 'Marx's opposition to capitalism was linked to his belief that exploitation was
immoral.' Discuss.
4 Does the commitment to revolution and class war prevent Marxists from taking
morality seriously?
5 Do you agree with the argument that Communist parties are just as elitist as
other political parties?

Guidance
Question 1
There are two reasons why a belief in historical inevitability has authoritarian consequences for Marxism. The first relates to the question of the so-called 'bourgeois
revolution' and the second links to the need for solidarity with ventures that may be
problematic in all kinds of ways.

Take the problem of the 'bourgeois revolution'. Because socialism is inevitable,
Marxists argue that other revolutions bring socialism ever closer and therefore should
be supported. This means that even revolutions that do not have the realisation of
socialism as their objective should be supported. Yet this can mean that revolutions
seeking to install middle-class leaders need to be supported, even though these
revolutions might become bogged down in corruption and repressive practices that
discredit socialism and might even place socialists themselves in personal jeopardy.

Revolutions that do call themselves socialist have also to be supported, since these
constitute part of historical experience, and are made in the name of the working

class. Yet like the Paris Commune, these revolutions may be hopeless attempts to achieve the impossible; or like the Bolshevik Revolution, can only survive through authoritarian political practices and human rights abuses. This being inevitable, how can one criticise it? Socialists then find themselves having to defend the indefensible on the grounds that such activities are somehow decreed by the historical process.

Question 2

It could be argued that Marx and Engels believed that socialism was only possible when the 'contradictions' of a capitalist society had reached boiling point. Socialists would inherit not only the technology of a developed capitalist society, but the liberal political culture and institutions as well. It is true that Marx and Engels became interested (towards the end of their lives) in a Russian revolution, but they always took the view that such a revolution could only be 'bourgeois' in character, and would spark socialist revolutions in mature capitalist societies. They cannot therefore be held responsible for what happened in Russia, eastern Europe and China, since these revolutions took place in conditions that were very different from those that Marx and Engels felt were necessary for socialism.

On the other hand, the revolutions that occurred in 1917 and beyond were not only made in the name of Marxism, but built upon certain authoritarian tendencies within Marx and Engels's own theories. The idea that socialism can only come about through the polarisation of class interests, that it requires a revolution and that it needs to be defended through a dictatorship of the proletariat encouraged the kind of authoritarian politics that was central to the Communist Party states.

Question 3

Marx certainly regarded capitalism as an immoral system. *Das Kapital* is full of searing indictments of the inhumanity and callousness of capitalist society, and other Marxist texts contain a fierce denunciation of the hypocrisy and cruelty of the capitalists. Moreover, it was not just liberal capitalism that was a target for Marx's wrath. Slavery and colonialism were condemned, and much was made of the terrible price that humanity had to pay for its progress through exploitation.

But Marx was also anxious not to appear 'purely' moralistic in his attitude towards capitalism and exploitation. In the *Communist Manifesto*, for example, he and Engels praise capitalism for demolishing feudal hierarchies and creating the basis of a cosmopolitan outlook and economy. Capitalism is also lauded because it unwittingly creates the basis for socialism, so that what makes exploitation immoral is that it ultimately holds humanity back. There are no 'abstract' principles that enable us to judge. Capitalism becomes immoral when it works against civilisation and progress. It is not inherently problematical.

Task 3.2 (continued)

Question 4

Revolutions involve polarisation and injustice. Even when revolution is justified because people are prevented from bringing about change through constitutional and peaceful means, it inevitably involves human rights abuses.

Marxism not only tends to glorify revolutions, but it argues the case for revolution in a liberal capitalist society. It is true that Marx conceded that revolutions need not always be violent. In societies where workers had won democratic rights, revolution could be peaceful and legal, although the argument for accepting constitutional forms of change was always tactical, i.e. legal protest was the best way of bringing about revolutionary change. This means that morality is always linked to class interests and it becomes tempting to argue that what serves the interests of the workers is moral, and what obstructs it is immoral. Opponents of socialism are seen as the enemy, and the idea of a war between the classes means that what helps your side is good and what aids the others is bad.

It is true that morality has to be linked to circumstances. Thus it can be deemed moral for a partisan during the Second World War to kill a Nazi, but it does not follow that innocent people mistaken for Nazi sympathisers can also be legitimately killed. The notion of revolution and class war lead to attitudes that ignore the right of humans in general to live peaceful and fulfilling lives.

Question 5

The Communist Party, as presented in classical Marxism, is deemed to be a self-dissolving entity. Workers need to support a communist party in order to spearhead a revolution and bring about a society that is not only classless, but free from repressive hierarchies as well, like the state and militant political parties. In theory, at any rate, Communist parties will become redundant in a society in which people can govern their own lives, and statist-type organisations no longer have any reason to exist.

But the *Communist Manifesto* argues that the role of Communists is to provide leadership, since they can see the totality of struggle. The formulations sound somewhat elitist, and Marxism, in its Leninist and later Stalinist formulations, saw the position of the Communist Party as a vanguard organisation. In Communist Party states membership of the party was obligatory if people wanted to enjoy recognition and success, and members of the party enjoyed privileges and special powers. Communist parties became just as elitist as any other political party, and right-wing radicals like Robert Michels saw in Bolshevism, for example, confirmation of his theory that all organisations are oligarchical: whatever their claims to democracy, they are run by, and in the interests of, minorities.

Useful websites

- www.marxist.org.uk/htm_docs/princip2.htm
- www.spartacus.schoolnet.co.uk
- www.socialistparty.org.uk/russia/r2frame.htm?stalin.html

Further reading

- Crick, B. (1987) *Socialism*, Open University Press.
- Hunt, R. N. (1974) *The Political Ideas of Marx and Engels*, University of Pittsburgh Press.
- Kolakowski, L. (1978) *Main Current of Marxism*, Oxford University Press.
- Lenin, V. I. (1918) *The State and Revolution*, in *Collected Works*, Vol. 25, Progress, 1964.
- Lenin, V. I. (1920) *Left-wing Communism: An Infantile Disorder*, in *Collected Works*, Vol. 31, Progress, 1966.
- Marx, K. (1871) *The Civil War in France*, in *Marx/Engels Seclected Works*, Progress, 1968.

THE HENLEY COLLEGE LIBRARY

What is democratic socialism?

We have seen the problem of Marxism as an authoritarian socialism. Socialists have generally rejected a revolutionary model and committed themselves to liberal democratic institutions. This kind of socialism has been greatly influential in Britain and in western Europe.

A terminological question

Up until 1914 (as noted above) the term 'social democrat' was widely adopted. It was used by both the Bolsheviks and the British Labour Party. In 1914 a great schism occurred. Some socialists supported the First World War, and this divide was deepened when the Bolshevik Revolution took place in 1917. Although socialists generally welcomed the fall of tsarism in March 1917, many, including those who considered themselves Marxists, saw the seizure of power by Lenin

Illustrated London News

Soldiers with the red flag attached to their bayonets during the Russian Revolution of 1917

in October 1917 as the act of madman, a *coup d'état* rather than a genuine revolution, a premature act which ignored the 'unripe' conditions in Russia.

From then on, the concept of a social democrat became a term of differentiation, with the emphasis now on *democracy*. Socialists who opposed the Russian Revolution, and subsequent Leninist and Stalinist rule, invariably called themselves democratic socialists — a term we shall use interchangeably with social democrat.

Socialism as opposed to communism

Socialism, it was argued, must differentiate itself from communism. It is concerned with reforms, not revolution: it must develop through parliamentary democracy, not through workers' councils or soviets. It must express itself through electoral victory, not a seizure of power: nor should socialists tie themselves to the leadership of the working class. Socialism involves the whole nation — not simply a part of it — and socialism must be realistic, attained through piecemeal reforms and in a manner that works with, and respects, the liberal tradition. As the French socialist Jean Jaurès put it, 'the great majority of the nation can be won over to our side by propaganda and lawful action and led to socialism'.

Social democracy sees itself as everything that Marxism is not: democratic, reformist, realistic, open-minded and concerned with the moral case for socialism.

The identity problem

Socialism, as presented above, does have a problem. It is so anti-utopian that it is vulnerable to the charge that it is no different in essence from liberalism and even more flexible versions of conservatism. Is it a movement in its own right? Berki makes the point that, just as in Aristotle aristocracy can turn into its degenerate form, oligarchy, so social democracy can turn into its degenerate form, which is electoralism, i.e. a concern to win elections without worrying about principles at all.

In other words, social democracy suffers from a serious identity problem. It is so pragmatic and flexible, so concerned with avoiding divisiveness and outraging — as the social democratic writer Durbin puts it, 'the conservative sections of all classes' — that it becomes a form of conservatism itself (or liberalism) and cannot be called socialism at all. Socialism, we have argued, is vulnerable to the charge of utopianism: but a forthright rebuttal of utopianism of any kind may mean that the transformative element in socialism is lost, and socialism 'degenerates'.

Eduard Bernstein and the German socialists

Eduard Bernstein (1850–1932) is a significant figure to examine, for his critique of classical Marxism formed the theory and practice of what came to be called social democracy. He influenced a tradition that was resistant to theory. In his work, social democracy is not only contrasted explicitly and in detail with Marxism, but its own premises are lucidly displayed. Indeed, the book that has the English title of *Evolutionary Socialism* was actually called (if one translates the German directly) *The Premises of Socialism and the Task of Social Democracy.*

Eduard Bernstein

Bernstein joined the German socialists in 1872. When the warring groups united, the party went from electoral success to electoral success. In 1876 it won 9% of the votes cast. Bismarck, the German chancellor, used the attempt to assassinate the emperor (not, it should be said, by socialists) to harass the party. Bernstein, who was in Switzerland at the time, became converted to Marxism.

Despite the problems caused by Bismarck's anti-socialist law (which only lapsed in 1890), the party polled 12% of the vote in the elections of 1881. In 1884 the party sent 24 members to the Reichstag (the German parliament). Under renewed pressure from Bismarck, Bernstein was forced to leave Switzerland, and went to London. In 1890 the party secured nearly 20% of the vote in the national elections and increased its number of MPs to 35. By 1903 the SPD (the Social Democratic Party of Germany) had 81 seats in its parliament.

Bernstein, revisionism and the British tradition

Engels, who died in 1895, had already expressed his concern for Bernstein's enthusiasm for the Fabians — British socialists who explicitly rejected Marxism and named themselves after the Roman emperor Fabius, famed for his step-by-step approach to fighting war. Engels was to accuse the Fabians (whose society was established in London in 1874) of 'hushing up the class struggle'.

Bernstein was impressed by the tolerance and liberalism he found in London — so much so that Karl Kautsky (1854–1938), then the great champion of Marxist orthodoxy, was to declare Bernstein 'a representative of English socialism'. In a review of the German socialist Bebel's reminiscences, Bernstein mentions going to a charity entertainment event for the widow of a Paris Communard. At the top of the subscription list was a donation from Queen Victoria. If Marx had mellowed in Britain, 'why shouldn't I?', he seemed to have reasoned.

In 1899 Bernstein wrote his *Evolutionary Socialism* — described as the 'bible of revisionism'. Bernstein had been asked by Engels to be one of the executors of the Marxist papers, and Bernstein was reluctant to accept that he had — in the theological jargon that Marxists embrace — 'revised' Marxism. He argued that his critique was a way of further developing Marxism: he was not destroying Marxism, since, as he put it, 'It is Marx who carries the point against Marx.' But what he argued was certainly explosive, and a different kind of socialism emerged in his critique.

Bernstein's argument

Bernstein's view can be summed up as follows.
- Small and medium enterprises were proving themselves viable. Hence members of the possessing classes were increasing, not diminishing. Society was not becoming more simplified (as the *Communist Manifesto* declared), but more graduated and differentiated. Moreover, the constantly rising national product was distributed — albeit unequally — over all segments of the population, so that the position of the worker was improving. In agriculture, the small and medium landholding was increasing, and the large and very large decreasing.
- Bernstein followed the Fabians by arguing that the theory of value or surplus value in Marxist theory was unnecessary. Depressions were becoming milder.

Modern banking and the internationalisation of trade created adjustment and flexibility in capitalism — not breakdown.

- He saw Marx's emphasis on dialectics (the view that the world consists of opposing forces) as a snare, uncritically taken over from Hegel. Why not assume that cooperation is just as important as struggle? Socialism must be based on the facts, and it is a fact that there is compromise and cooperation between the classes.
- Ethical factors, in Bernstein's view, create much greater space for independent activity than was seen to be the case in classical Marxism. The notion of inevitability — a fusion of what is and what ought to be — must be decisively rejected. 'No ism is a science.' Socialism is about what is ethically desirable: science is about what is.
- Democracy, for Bernstein, is 'an absence of class government' — it avoids both the tyranny of the majority and the tyranny of the minority. Democracy is the high school of compromise and moderation. The notion of the 'dictatorship of the proletariat' has become redundant. Socialism seeks to make the proletarian into a citizen 'and to thus make citizenship universal'.
- Socialism, declared Bernstein, is 'the legitimate heir' to liberalism 'as a great historical movement'. There is no really liberal thought that does not also belong to socialism. Industrial courts and trades councils involve democratic self-government. Socialism is 'organising liberalism' and requires the constant increase of municipal freedom. Bernstein was devoted to liberal parliamentarism, and if this parliamentarism becomes excessive, the antidote is local self-government.
- The SPD must fight for all those reforms that increase the power of the workers and give the state a more democratic form. Bernstein described the SPD as a 'democratic-Socialist reform party'. Hence the trade unions, far from being schools for socialism (in Marx's revolutionary sense), were concerned with practical and non-revolutionary improvements. Trade unions are, declared Bernstein, 'indispensable organs of democracy'.
- Bernstein linked the practicality of trade unions with the empirical orientation of the cooperative movement. The class struggle continues, but it is taking ever-milder forms. Cooperatives, particularly consumer co-ops, encourage democratic and egalitarian forms of management.
- Bernstein exemplifies what can be described as the dilemma of democratic socialism. How can the social democratic party navigate between what Gay in his book on Bernstein, *The Dilemma of Democratic Socialism* (1962), called 'the Scylla of impotence and the Charybidis of betrayal of its cause'? How can it be 'realistic' and yet remain socialist?

Box 4.1
Classical Marxism vs Eduard Bernstein

Marxism	Bernstein
dialectics	cooperation
concentration of capital	proliferation of small enterprises
inevitability	desirability
workers' councils	parliament
dictatorship of the proletariat	liberal democracy
nationalisation	cooperatives
revolution	reform

Conclusion

We use the term social democracy interchangeably with democratic socialism, and these terms only became distinct from Marxist versions of socialism after the First World War and the Bolshevik Revolution. Social democracy is identified with Eduard Bernstein's famous critique of classical Marxism, where he argued that the central theses of Marxism were contradicted by historical realities. By linking socialism much more sympathetically to liberalism, social democrats created a dilemma about the very identity of socialism: is democratic socialism a movement in its own right or is it indistinguishable from social liberalism and liberal conservatism?

Summary

- Before 1917 the term 'social democrat' had applied to socialist and Communist alike. It came to be used as a term of differentiation, with social democrats stressing that they were social *democrats*.
- Socialism is to be a doctrine of reforms, to be achieved gradually through parliamentary elections.
- The key theorist of democratic socialism is Eduard Bernstein, who spent part of his political life in Britain and was much influenced by the liberalism and socialism he encountered there.
- Bernstein's *Evolutionary Socialism* argues that socialism must reject classical Marxist notions of inevitability, revolution, class war, capitalist depression, the dictatorship of the proletariat and anti-utopianism.
- Social democracy is so concerned with being realistic that it appears, according to its critics, to have ceased to be a legitimate form of socialism at all.

Task 4.1

Read the passage below and answer the question that follows.

Ditching Clause IV from the Labour Party

The old Clause IV, which was enshrined in the 1918 constitution of the British Labour Party, declared that its objective was 'to secure for the workers by hand and by brain the full fruits of their industry and the most equitable distribution thereof that may be possible on the basis of the common ownership of the means of production, distribution and exchange, and the best obtainable system of popular administration and control of each industry and service'.

To many Labour Party members this clause stood as evidence of a true socialist commitment, since common ownership meant public ownership. In 1959 the party leader, Hugh Gaitskell, sought to remove the clause from Labour's constitution, but he was defeated by the party conference. To those on the 'right', Clause IV was an embarrassing and fundamentalist assertion that was impractical and a gift to Labour's ideological opponents. It was all very well to speak of 'popular administration', but didn't Clause IV suggest the kind of wholesale nationalisation that was incompatible with liberal democracy and appeared to echo the authoritarian system of socialism that existed in eastern Europe? It was a commitment that bedevilled the democratic credentials of the Labour Party.

In 1995 Tony Blair, just a year after becoming party leader, secured the removal of the old Clause IV and replaced it by a new Clause IV that asserted a belief that 'by the strength of our common endeavour we achieve more than we achieve alone, so as to create for each of us the means to realise our true potential and for all of us a community in which wealth, power and opportunity are in the hands of the many, not the few'. The new Clause IV preferred the notion of community to 'common ownership', asserting that we need a society where 'we live together, freely, in a spirit of solidarity, tolerance and respect'. In Blair's view the old clause was unworkable and was never intended to be implemented; the new clause, it is argued, brings Labour in line with the values of social democracy, and the fact, as the new Clause IV asserts, that Labour 'is a democratic socialist party'.

Question

Should the Labour Party have given up its original Clause IV?

Guidance

Arguments in favour

• The original clause seemed to suggest that nationalisation of the means of production was the ultimate object of the Labour Party, however gradualist and constitutional its methods. This implied that, although the Labour Party distanced

Task 4.1 (continued)

itself from Marxism, it hankered after the same kind of 'state socialism' that characterised the Communist Party states.

- The old Clause IV was a propagandist gift to the opponents of Labour. Introduced by the Webbs (Fabian thinkers who were very influential in moulding the Labour Party) to put clear (red) water between Labour and the Tories, it was an archaic ideological symbol that was vague, unworkable and threatening.
- Labour prides itself on being a democratic socialist party imbued with the spirit of liberalism. Clause IV appeared illiberal and encouraged fundamentalist aspirations that were inconsistent with this liberal ethos, and had a distinct totalitarian ring to it.

Arguments against

- Clause IV represented a genuine socialist value. It is wrong to think of nationalisation as necessarily implying top-down state control. Public ownership simply means community control, and a policy that strengthens a democratic society.
- Workers have a collective identity born of labouring in factories and surviving through cooperation. Clause IV recognised this collectivism and underlined the objective of moving beyond capitalist attitudes and institutions.
- Clause IV indicated that although the political methods of Labour are gradualist, constitutional and democratic, its ends are just as socialist as those espoused by revolutionary parties. In fact, its ends are more socialist because the methods taken to reach them are practical and correspond to the everyday experience of millions of people.

Task 4.2

Using this chapter and other resources available to you, answer the following questions:

1 Why do social democrats present their doctrine as a democratic socialism?
2 Is democratic socialism an authentic form of socialism, or is it simply social liberalism by another name?
3 Was Bernstein a Marxist?
4 Why did social democrats oppose the idea that revolution was inevitable?
5 'Bernstein made socialism electorally viable.' Discuss.

Guidance
Question 1
Historically, the term 'social democrat' was adopted by all socialists, whether they were Marxists or not, on the grounds that liberal democracy has brought political rights, but

Task 4.2 (continued)

what was required was the social power and equality to make democracy a reality. Bolsheviks called themselves social democrats, as did more liberal-minded socialists.

The First World War and the Russian Revolution changed all this. Marxists argued that the leaders of the Second Socialist International had betrayed the interests of workers by supporting the war and opposing the Bolshevik Revolution. In order to differentiate themselves from 'reformists' and 'traitors', Marxists called themselves Communists, and set up Communist parties in opposition to established socialist parties. The leaders of these socialist parties retaliated by arguing that they were democrats who repudiated the dictatorial methods and doctrinaire policies of the Communists, so that the emphasis was now placed upon the 'democratic' rather than the 'socialist' part of the label.

Of course, Marxists generally rejected the concept of 'democratic socialist' as a term for evolutionary, parliamentary socialists on the grounds that they believed in democracy as well: in fact, in a democracy that was far more democratic than the liberal version that the 'reformists' supported.

Question 2

It is true that democratic socialists saw in liberal institutions values and virtues that revolutionary socialists did not. In Britain they formed close links with the Liberal Party and were gratified when new liberals like Leonard Hobhouse were quite happy to describe themselves as socialists as well as liberals. Even J. S. Mill, often seen as a quintessentially liberal thinker, had declared himself a socialist, and presented a social view of freedom.

But it would be wrong to see democratic socialists as simply social liberals. Bernstein had referred to socialism as 'organising liberalism' and socialists saw themselves as resolving the gulf between theory and practice that afflicted all liberals, even 'new' ones. Social liberals, after all, sought to humanise capitalism — they wanted reforms but they did not want a new system of society. They believed that the state should intervene in order to enable more people to own their own property and benefit from the market. Democratic socialists, on the other hand, saw and see their objective as one of changing human nature and developing a more cooperative world. Certainly democratic socialism is close to social liberalism, but it is also distinct. It seeks ultimately to transform capitalism rather than to make it fairer.

Question 3

Bernstein had been appointed as the executor of Marx and Engels's works and he regarded himself as a Marxist. Indeed, he argued in his famous 'revisionist' work that history had changed, and since Marxism was concerned with adapting socialist values to historical realities, his own work accorded with a Marxist methodology and outlook.

Task 4.2 (continued)

The problem, of course, is that Bernstein challenged the fundamental postulates of classical Marxist theory. Philosophically, he rejected dialectics and materialism; politically, he argued passionately against the notion of class war, revolution and the dictatorship of the proletariat — he saw the idea of a classless and stateless society as fanciful and unrealisable; and economically, he opposed Marx's notion of exploitation and surplus value.

Question 4

Some social democrats argued that the nation was sliding to gradualism, and that such was the logic of socialism that society would find change irresistible. But the notion of inevitability here is tied to the concept of evolution. It was linked to the belief that the facts pointed increasingly to the need for social regulation and state intervention, so that more and more people would support social democratic policies.

But the idea that revolution is inevitable was seen by social democrats as dogmatic and wrong-headed. Revolution would only arise where the mass of the population had no way of changing institutions peacefully and legally, and given the fact that people had political rights, they could and should use these to bring about sensible and sustainable change. It was not true that capitalism increasingly divided people so that polarisation mounted and the gulf between rich and poor worsened. Capitalism was not the kind of homogenous system about which Marxists spoke. On the contrary, it was being steadily socialised — through recognising trade unions, establishing cooperatives and introducing social reforms — so that people were living together more harmoniously and seeing that they had important interests in common. This was not only true within countries — it was also true between countries. Fabians advocated a notion of world community in which wealth could be more fairly shared, cultural differences respected, and trade could be used as a way of helping poorer countries to progress.

Question 5

Bernstein had been influenced by the increasing representation of the German socialists in the German parliament (the Reichstag). Of course, elections meant that socialists could only implement policies that had widespread popular support, and they had to avoid short cuts and dramatic changes engineered from above by leaders who claimed to understand the 'real' interests of people as opposed to their momentary opinions.

Bernstein was concerned with practical politics, although he is vulnerable to the charge of clinging to parliamentary traditions even when (as with the rise of the Nazis) these were being abandoned by millions of people who were disillusioned with liberalism and had turned to the right. Parliamentary socialism presupposes

Task 4.2 (continued)

liberal political institutions, but it does mean that people have to be convinced that policies are correct. By stressing the importance of reforms, Bernstein made socialism workable and relevant, and by seeing democracy as the school of compromise he stressed the importance of convincing the majority of people that change was possible and desirable.

Marxists flourished where liberal institutions were either absent or worked badly so that people regarded elections as irrelevant or farcical. Bernstein took the view that even the wealthy could see that if they were intransigent they would lose everything: like the poor, they would respect electoral verdicts they did not like, on the grounds that they would have an opportunity to have a government in the future that was more to their liking.

Useful websites

- www.spartacus.schoolnet.co.uk
- http://en.wikipedia.org/wiki/EduardBernstein

Further reading

- Berki, R. (1974) *Socialism*, Dent.
- Bernstein, E. (1899) *Evolutionary Socialism*.
- Gay, P. (1962) *The Dilemma of Democratic Socialism*, Collier Books.

Is the British Labour Party socialist?

The British Labour Party has never been a party of theory. Although its members (and some of its leaders!) may not even have heard of Bernstein, it is Bernsteinism that provides the underpinning for its practice.

Problems with the Liberal Party

In the last quarter of the nineteenth century, disillusionment with the British liberals under the leadership of Gladstone was mounting. Political and social reforms seemed to have run out of steam, and policies abroad were imperialistic. In particular, the support for coercion in Ireland aroused deep misgivings. The American radical Henry George captured this dis-content in his attack on landlordism in *Progress and Poverty* (1879).

In 1884 Hyndman founded the Social Democratic Federation (SDF). In 1887 a demonstration for free speech was broken up by the police in Trafalgar Square on 'Bloody Sunday'. Despite the authoritarian leadership of Hyndman, the SDF controlled the London Trades Council and provided, in the words of historian Eric Hobsbawm, 'a training school for the most gifted of the working class militants'.

Illustrated London News

'Bloody Sunday': Trafalgar Square, 13 November 1887

The Fabians

The importance of the Fabians has already been mentioned. The Fabian Society became a kind of think-tank for the Labour Party. It had emerged out of the Ethical Fellowship for the New Life. Drawing upon Victorian radicalism, and a belief in historical change, the Fabians were influenced by the same kind of theories that so appealed to Bernstein — empiricism, a philosophy that argues that our knowledge comes through the observation of 'facts'; and a belief in piecemeal reform through parliamentary democracy. They saw capitalism as unjust and inefficient, and Sidney Webb declared that 'the economic side of the democratic ideal is, in fact, Socialism itself'. The primary aim of the society was to convince people, and especially people of influence, that the facts pointed to the practicality of socialism.

Socialism is not a philosophy of life, but a highly focused doctrine that concerns itself with the organisation of industry and the distribution of wealth. Examine Fabian pamphlets today and what do you find? Specific proposals on organising the civil service, the health service, tax reforms, social security benefits, European Monetary Union and the like. Beatrice Webb (1858–1943), who played a key role in the Fabian Society and in the formation of the Labour Party, took the view that the whole nation was sliding towards social democracy.

The birth of the Labour Party

The Trades Union Congress was created in 1868 and 3 years later the Parliamentary Committee was formed. By 1886 there were nine workingmen in Parliament, sitting as 'Lib-Labs' (trade unionists who supported the Liberal Party). Resentment brewed at the elitist attitude that these MPs had towards the unskilled workers and the great Dock Strike occurred in 1889. 'New' unionism, organising the unskilled, flourished, and Engels was moved to comment that 'the masses are on the move'.

In 1892 Keir Hardie (1856–1915) was elected to the Commons, and a year later formed the Independent Labour Party. The Labour Representative Committee (LRC) was created in 1900 by trade unions alarmed by the proliferation of employers' associations and a decision by the Appeal Court drastically to limit the right of picketing. The Taff Vale case,

Illustrated London News

Keir Hardie

which left the unions liable for damages in the event of a strike, saw a substantial increase in union support for the LRC: these unions felt that they needed a political voice and would cooperate with any party engaged in promoting legislation 'in the direct interest of labour'. The Liberal Party did not oppose the two Labour candidates who won their seats in by-elections in 1902 and 1903.

Labour and the trade unions

Twenty-nine LRC candidates were returned in 1906, and a Trades Dispute Act was passed which strengthened the right of unions to strike. In 1908 the Eight-Hour Act was passed. In 1909 the House of Lords declared that it was illegal for a trade union to contribute financially to a political party, but the Trade Union Act of 1913 allowed the trade unions to affiliate to the Labour Party. In the election of 1910, 42 Labour candidates had been returned to office and Ramsay MacDonald (1866–1937), the party leader, made it clear that political weapons were to be found in the ballot box and the Act of Parliament — not in collective bargaining.

During the First World War the TUC agreed to suspend strike action and restrictive practices, and Henderson, who had taken over from MacDonald as party leader, joined the War Cabinet. Henderson, MacDonald and Sidney Webb created a constitution for the party in 1918 and the famous Clause IV, which spoke of common ownership of the means of production, was (rather cynically) inserted to give the party some kind of ideological distance from the Conservatives and the Liberals. As Tony Blair commented in 1995, Sidney Webb would have been astonished to find that the clause was still in existence some 70 years later. It was not intended, Blair argued, to be taken seriously.

The Labour Party under Ramsay MacDonald

Illustrated London News

Labour had become a national party, and the 1922 programme made it clear that Labour stood for neither Bolshevism nor communism, but 'common sense and justice'. In the 1924 election Labour formed a minority government with Ramsay MacDonald as prime minister — a man described by Beatrice Webb, one of the great Fabian thinkers,

Ramsay MacDonald in 1924

as 'a believer in individualist political democracy tempered in its expression by Utopian Socialism'.

The new Labour government failed to tackle the problem of unemployment, but its loan to Russia was seized upon by Liberals and Tories as evidence of the government's pro-Communist leanings. With the publication of the forged Zinoviev letter (calling for armed insurrection in Britain) the government fell. In the wake of the collapse of the General Strike, the Conservative government passed another Trade Union Act that made trade unionists 'contract in' if they wanted to support the Labour Party.

Guards returning from Hackney and the London Docks after the General Strike of 1926

Illustrated London News

The expulsion of Ramsay MacDonald

In 1929 Labour came to power once again, but an inability to tackle the growing unemployment crisis led to the resignation of MacDonald and the formation of a National Government in 1931, as a result of which MacDonald was expelled from the Labour Party.

It is true that it suited the Liberals and Conservatives to present Labour as, in Churchill's words, 'the party of revolution', but in fact Labour's politics were always of a liberal and constitutional nature. It is revealing that during the crisis of 1931 the Tory leader, Sir Herbert Samuel, argued that it would be in the general interest if unpalatable social measures to deal with the economic crisis could be imposed by a Labour government. In the 1930s the Labour leadership was opposed to the Popular Front government in Spain, and contributed significantly to the appeasement of the extreme right.

Labour's pragmatism

Although the right-wing publicist Evelyn Waugh saw the country after the Labour electoral victory of 1945 as being under occupation, in fact Morrison, acting leader of the party in 1945, made it clear that the socialisation of industry would only work 'on the merits of their specific cases. That is how the British mind works. It does not work in a vacuum or in abstract theories.'

There is a clear link between the Fabian theoretician Sidney Webb's statement to the Labour conference of 1923 that the founder of British socialism was not 'Karl Marx but Robert Owen — the doctrine underlying the party is not that of class war but human brotherhood' — and Harold Wilson's comment at the 1966 conference that no answers are to be found in Highgate cemetery (i.e. where Marx is buried).

The birth of 'New Labour'

Following the victory of Margaret Thatcher in 1979 the Labour Party was paralysed by internal squabbles between left and right — although it should be noted that Tony Benn, a major opponent of the 'right wing', always considered himself a democratic socialist. The 1983 election programme was famously described as 'the longest suicide note in history'. Neil Kinnock was elected leader and began to 'reform' the party. He was replaced by John Smith after 1992, and Tony Blair took over as party leader after Smith's death in 1994.

Blair's socialism

The position of Tony Blair follows the tradition of pragmatism, moralism and constitutionalism. Indeed, Blair makes it clear that the elimination of the old Clause IV was to facilitate a return to Labour's ethical roots. We must retain, he argues, the values and principles underlying democratic socialism but apply them entirely afresh to the modern world.

The values of democratic socialism are 'social justice, the equal worth of each citizen, equality of opportunity, community'. Socialism is, if you will, social-ism. In a lecture to mark the fiftieth anniversary of the 1945 Labour victory, Blair described socialism as 'the political heir of radical liberalism'. He sees the New Liberals as

Tony Blair

social democrats, and he defines socialism as a form of politics through which to fight poverty, prejudice and unemployment, and to create the conditions in which to build one nation — tolerant, fair, enterprising and inclusive. Socialists have to be both moralists and empiricists. They need, on the one hand, to be concerned with values, but at the same time they must address themselves to a world as it is and not as we would like it to be.

The third way

The notion of the third way had traditionally been used to suggest a route that was neither capitalist nor Stalinist. Now it was used to point to policies that were supposedly critical of capitalism and also of the 'conservatism' of traditional Labour attitudes.

The third way involves devising policies that are acceptable to what is considered to be 'middle England'. If voters in middle England are unhappy with high taxation, then Labour must ditch policies that would increase taxes. If people in middle England are devoted to the tabloid press, then Labour must ensure that they have the tabloids on their side. If middle England is concerned with acquiring more wealth than its neighbours in the north, then aspirations to greater equality must be dropped.

The notion of morality must be re-emphasised so that New Labour sees the family and schools as traditional purveyors of the distinction between right and wrong. Critics of the third way argue that in practice, the traditional values of social democracy have been replaced by a kind of Thatcherite 'socialism' that rejects equality, embraces privatisation and the market, and encourages elitism and a contempt for Parliament and discussion. The decision to go to war against Iraq is seen as a dramatic failure to maintain an independent foreign policy and led to the late Robin Cook leaving the cabinet.

Box 5.1			
Labour leaders			
Hardie	1906–08	Attlee	1935–55
Henderson	1908–10	Gaitskell	1955–63
Barnes	1910–11	Wilson	1963–76
MacDonald	1911–14	Callaghan	1976–80
Henderson	1914–17	Foot	1980–83
Adamson	1917–21	Kinnock	1983–92
Clynes	1921–22	Smith	1992–94
MacDonald	1922–31	Blair	1994– 2007

International social democrats

Social democratic notions (though not necessarily the particular views of Blair) have been internationally endorsed. The German SPD (Social Democratic Party) has sternly repudiated communism, and in its Bad Godesburg Resolution of 1959 — described by Berki as 'one of the boldest, most impressive "liberal" party manifestoes ever written' — it argues for competition where possible, planning 'as far as it is necessary'. It follows what the Swedish social democrats have called a 'matter-of-fact conception of man'.

These comments capture the dilemma. Berki suggests that in a way social democracy can be characterised as 'utopian socialism minus utopian expectations' since it does not believe that ideals like justice, goodwill, brotherliness and compassion can be 'unreservedly realised'. Is social democracy so pragmatic and flexible that it cannot be called socialism at all?

Conclusion

The British Labour Party arose out of the Labour Representation Committee, and its roots demonstrated its pragmatism and the centrality of the trade unions. The party never accepted Marxism as its guiding philosophy, and left its theorising to groups like the Fabian Society. Although its opponents accused it of extremism, it clung to moderate policies. True, it expelled MacDonald, the party leader who formed a coalition government with the Conservatives in the 1930s. Blair has considered the tradition of moralism and pragmatism as central to Labour Party values, although his critics have felt that he has strayed from social democracy and become a Tory in his policies and attitudes.

Summary

- The birth of the British Labour Party was facilitated by the decline of the Liberal Party in the late nineteenth century when Liberal policies seemed increasingly unable to handle the stresses and strains of an industrialised society and a colonial world.
- The tone and focus of Labour Party politics was set by the Fabian Society. Fabians saw themselves as practical political thinkers, dealing with specific problems and using a specific expertise.
- The formation of the Labour Representation Committee as a precursor to the Labour Party was made possible by trade union fears that the Liberals could no longer ensure that trade union-friendly legislation was secured.

- Labour cooperated closely with the Liberals, joined a coalition government during the First World War and formed a government in 1922. It fell 2 years later as a result of the Zinoviev letter.
- Labour's moderation was not infinite, and the expulsion of MacDonald from the party in 1931 shows that Labour's loyalties were of significance. The victory of 1945 saw a reforming Labour government that alarmed the right.
- The influence of left-wing perspectives around Benn saw the marginalisation of the party with the rise of New Labour under Blair as an attempt to restore the party's electoral fortunes. The third way has not only re-emphasised traditional social democratic themes: it has embraced an agenda that many of its critics feel has abandoned socialist values even in their most moderate form.
- New Labour has aggravated the problem that affects social democracy in general: its identity crisis. If pragmatism and realism are carried too far, can social democracy be said to have any socialist credentials at all?

Task 5.1

Consider the following quotation from Ramsay MacDonald and answer the questions that follow.

> Socialism cannot succeed while it is a mere creed; it must become a movement. And it cannot become a movement until two things happen. It must be the organising power behind a confluence of forces each of which is converging upon it, but not all of which actually profess it as a consciously held belief; it must also gain the confidence of the mass of the working class... The Labour Party is not socialist. It is a union of Socialist and trade-union bodies for immediate political work... But it is the only political form which evolutionary Socialism can take in a country with the political traditions and methods of Great Britain. Under British conditions, a Socialist Party is the last, not the first, form of the Socialist movement in politics.

From *The Socialist Movement*, 1911, cited by Crick, B. (1987) *Socialism*, Open University Press, p. 70

Questions

1 Is socialism a creed rather than a movement?

2 Is it correct to argue that the Labour Party is not socialist?

3 What influence do British political traditions have on the character of socialism in Britain?

4 'Evolutionary socialism is more practical than revolutionary socialism.' Discuss.

5 Can socialists combine everyday struggles with the vision of an alternative social order?

Task 5.1 (continued)

Guidance

- MacDonald argues that socialism is not a creed, but a movement. But is it not both? If it is only a creed, then it becomes a set of values that small numbers may embrace but which fail to make any impact upon society at large. But if it is only a movement, is there not a danger that socialism simply accommodates itself to the opinion of the day, even though this might not be in the interests of most men and women, and might be formulated by vested interests who can use the media and education system to their advantage?

- MacDonald is right to see the importance of changes that fall short of socialist ideas, but which move a situation forward and are supported by people who are not clear about the implications of these policies. Thus, to take a modern example, people might support a ban on smoking without being aware that this involves a break with traditional liberal conceptions of the individual and freedom.

- Is it correct to argue that the Labour Party is not a socialist party? The strength of this position is that it sees socialism as something towards which the party is moving, and therefore it would be wrong to expect the Labour Party to advocate socialist policies when these may seem irrelevant to the mass of the population. The weakness of this position is that it privileges means and ignores the ends, so that the party simply becomes concerned with everyday issues and neglects the long-term direction in which society needs to travel.

- By stressing the British character of parliamentary traditions, this could mean that when it comes to other countries liberal institutions need not apply. This might have two problematic consequences. The first is that autocracy in other countries is accepted on the grounds that their conditions differ from British ones, and therefore we would be wrong to criticise them. The second is that the British can rule other countries in a despotic fashion since parliamentary institutions are only relevant when British people are ruled. In other words, the statement might be seen as justification for appeasing foreign dictators and endorsing colonialism.

- Twenty years after these words were published, MacDonald dissolved his cabinet and formed a national coalition with the Conservatives. Despite the fact that he was Labour leader and prime minister, he was expelled from the party. It could be argued that the extremely pragmatic concept of socialism and party that he espouses here means that this development is not entirely surprising.

Task 5.2

Using this chapter and other resources available to you, answer the following questions:

1 Do disputes over the meaning of democratic socialism matter?

2 Why has the British Labour Party adopted an evolutionary rather than a revolutionary form of socialism?

3 'Social democracy has no identity of its own.' Discuss.

4 'The Labour Party can only humanise capitalism: it is incapable of changing it.' Discuss.

5 Do you agree with the proposition that under Blair's leadership, the Labour Party has abandoned its commitment to democratic socialism?

Guidance

Question 1

Critics of socialism claim that socialists embrace an argument for a planned and egalitarian society, and that such a society destroys individual freedoms, torpedoes choice and brings about inefficiency, chaos and autocracy. Democratic socialism is a contradiction in terms, however we define the notion.

On the other hand, it could be argued that the word 'democratic' in the description of a particular variant of socialism is important and the concept has an important bearing on the distinction between revolutionary and evolutionary socialism. Marxists argue that real democracy involves workers' councils and that liberal democracy is a fake form of democracy: it is democracy for the capitalists and ignores the interests of ordinary people even though the latter have the vote. Social democrats, however, take the view that revolution itself, when carried out (or even aimed at) in a liberal society, leads to the adoption of undemocratic practices, and that it is Leninist, Stalinist, Maoist or Trotskyist democracy that is fake and implausible. Unless democracy exists for everyone, it exists for no one, and although socialists take the view that liberal institutions 'on their own' are inadequate, they are a precondition nevertheless for a democratic society. There can be no democracy without a free press, the right to criticise and to form and support political parties of one's choosing.

It is true that social democrats may become so pragmatic that they become indistinguishable from liberals and even moderate conservatives, but that is not the fault (but rather a distortion) of democratic socialism.

Question 2

It is argued by its Marxist critics that the British Labour Party has embraced liberal ideas to the detriment of socialist values. It has a naïve view of the constitution,

Task 5.2 (continued)

legality and the state, and it plays down the way in which class and capitalism dominate society. It is also seen as the beneficiary of empire, displacing social divisions to the colonies and oblivious of the fact that the reforms at home have been made possible by the super-profits earned through investments abroad.

Yet the British Labour Party arose out of the demands of trade unions for a legal framework that made collective bargaining possible. Hence its name. But it is also a party that reaches out to the wider public, and enjoys some support among the wealthier sections of society as well. Whereas Communist parties have mostly come and gone, the British Labour Party wins elections, reforms society and makes a practical impact. It may not have the glamour of revolutionary parties, but it enjoys support and affection, and seeks to modernise its message and policies. An evolutionary form of socialism is relevant and viable, and although the question of socialism remains contentious within the party, few challenge its evolutionary strategy.

Question 3

Social democrats argue that they are practical and down to earth. They respect liberal institutions and because they win elections and form governments, they are able to carry through reforms that actually change people's lives for the better.

Their critics argue that social democrats are *so* concerned with being practical and realistic that the changes they make are trivial and at best marginal. Inequality continues, the domination of the state by the wealthy, the power of money and the market, the subordination of women and insecurity and racism. In Britain today it is sometimes argued that so conservative is the current Labour government that the Liberal Democrat Party seems more progressive and daring, and even the Conservatives take issue with the government's position on civil rights. What we see yet again is the failure of social democracy to challenge capitalism. It acts in an unprincipled and opportunist way, discredits socialism, and since it appears indistinguishable from its political rivals, loses the support of the electorate. If Marxists are drawn to authoritarianism, social democrats embrace a kind of opportunism that leads it to place survival above principles. Disillusionment follows and social democrats fall from office, losing the power even to introduce the kind of marginal and mild reforms they promise.

Question 4

The Labour Party is so fearful of being revolutionary and unconstitutional that it is unable to bring about the kind of change that would challenge capitalism and the power of the rich. Although it claims to be socialist, in practice it never does more than humanise capitalism, so that class divisions and class power remain intact.

Task 5.2 (continued)

This view has two problems with it. First of all, it fails to see that humanising capitalism is worthwhile. If workers have a minimum wage, enjoy stable economic conditions, get support for their families, have more human rights and can acquire information that they were never able to obtain before — these are important gains. The Scots now have their own parliament, so do the Welsh: these changes do not bring about a socialist as opposed to a capitalist society, but they could be seen as valuable democratic reforms.

But even more importantly, the argument that Labour is incapable of changing capitalism ignores the unintended consequences and the 'logic' that reforms can unleash. If workers have more rights, this increases their confidence and assertiveness. They begin to question as never before traditional values and customary capitalist prerogatives. Revolutions can be seen not as concentrated political events in which Bastilles are stormed and monarchs executed, but as changes in political culture and attitudes. Politicians may bring about changes that have far more profound repercussions than they realise. For example, addressing climate change or banning smoking have implications for freedom that, it could be argued, strengthen the 'logic' of collectivism and community — socialist rather than capitalist values.

Question 5

Blair has won unprecedented levels of electoral support as a moderniser. He has, say his admirers, brought the Labour Party into the twenty-first century, with a political style that is self-critical, sensitive to public opinion and refreshingly innovative. He has done much to increase a spirit of independence and entrepreneurship, showing that the market and capitalism can be used to democratise schooling, make the welfare state more efficient and reward people in a much fairer way.

His critics have produced a formidable case against him. They argue that he has failed to make society more equal and although he speaks of the need for community, in practice his policies have increased greed and corruption, and weakened collective identities and institutions. His foreign policy, far from being more ethical, has been disastrous, and his involvement in Iraq War has seen a catastrophic lack of open government, uniting millions of people from all walks of life against him. Politicians once seen on the Labour 'right', like Hattersley, are hostile to Blair and from being a dynamic and attractive political leader, he has become an electoral liability to the party that he rules in an increasingly autocratic and 'presidential' manner.

It is, however, important to make a distinction between Blair, as leader, and the Labour Party itself. It could be argued that members of the party remain committed to democratic socialist policies and values even though their leader does not.

Useful websites

- www.spartacus.schoolnet.co.uk
- www.labour.org.uk
- www.number-10.gov.uk/output/page4.asp

Further reading

- Adelman, P. (1986) *The Rise of the Labour Party, 1880-1945*, Longman.
- Berki, R. (1974) *Socialism*, Dent.
- Crick, B. (1987) *Socialism*, Open University.
- Miliband, R. (1973) *Parliamentary Socialism*, 2nd edn, Merlin.

What is the case against socialism?

The critics of socialism centre their arguments on the question of freedom. Socialism, they argue, is a step backwards — to the Middle Ages, when individual freedoms did not exist and people were dictated to by the communities and hierarchies to which they belonged. Liberals and conservatives disagree about many things, but they agree that socialism is a problematic movement and ideology that places society (and invariably the state) above the individual. Property is an expression of individual freedom and socialism, by bringing property under social (and state) control, necessarily threatens freedom.

The problem of planning

A major critic of socialism is Hayek (1899–1992). In Hayek's view, economic planning is the prime instrument of socialist reform. In *The Road to Serfdom* (1944) he tells us that he is not opposed to planning as such, if by planning we mean simply the handling of problems in a rational manner. Like the idea of organisation, day-to-day life requires the coordination of ends and means, but planning, as Hayek criticises it, aspires to the central direction of economic activity according to a single plan. This process is a recipe for disaster, since a modern economy involves an infinite number of choices and decisions, and the attempt to coordinate them can only be partial and highly imperfect.

In Hayek's view, economic planning always leads to anomalies since it is arrogantly seeking to do what is quite impossible. Suppressing the market leads to the kind of distortions that dramatically characterised the economies of eastern Europe when they were under Communist Party control — where a so-called 'black' or informal market sprang up in which people exchanged goods and services that were not catered for by the official institutions.

In praise of the market

The market requires the spontaneous and unplanned coordination of countless daily decisions, and the only way in which this process can work effectively is through competition. Of course, competition creates winners and losers, and leads to inequalities. But these are inherent in a civilised society and anti-socialists like Hayek certainly see the case for law and the state. The functioning of competition requires, in addition to a legal system, an adequate organisation of institutions like money, markets and the channels of information.

The system depends upon a respect for individuals, and this has to be enforced by the criminal law. Regulation is required to ensure that people abide by rules, but laws need to be general in the sense that they apply impartially to all. A competitive market system requires the rule of law, and the more complex society becomes, the more destructive is economic planning and the more relevant, competition.

Regulating competition

Hayek does not deny that competition between individual firms may lead to 'agreements' between firms that interfere with competition, and certain firms may become so dominant that they enjoy a position of monopoly.

But two things are important to note here. First, this process is often exaggerated and second, the problem needs to be tackled by using the legal process to increase competition, not snuff it out. The cultural and political consequences of the planning process are dire. Not only does inefficiency generate cynicism, but planners become godlike figures who inevitably exercise dictatorial control over people in general. The planners will necessarily not only interfere with the spontaneous processes of the economy, but will also be tempted to silence their critics. Hence planning leads to illiberal political practices as well, and Parliament is discredited if it tries to get involved in the planning process.

Those who lose out through ill health, unemployment, lack of skills etc. need to be helped, but the point is that such security must be provided outside the market, and competition be left to function unobstructed. The problem with the welfare state as it exists in contemporary liberal democracies, is that it undermines individual independence and responsibility, and corrupts the rule of law and an impartial system of government.

The position of democracy

In Hayek's view, democracy is not automatically desirable as a system of rule, since the people may pressurise their government to undermine markets, and indeed, the opposition of classical liberals to democracy was based precisely on the fear that people who had no or little private property would want an interventionist state and high levels of taxation.

But the fact is that socialism itself is incompatible with democracy since the planning process leads to the concentration of power in particular individuals, and by placing security above freedom, socialism leads to militarism and dictatorship. Values that socialism sacrifices are independence and self-reliance, individual initiative and local responsibility, non-interference with one's neighbour, toleration of the different, respect for custom and tradition, and a healthy suspicion of power and authority.

Community and state

Socialists see the community or state as prior to the individual. Socialism stresses the particular at the expense of the general, and despite its internationalist pretensions, socialism encourages nationalism and even imperialism.

It is impossible to respect people as individuals if the planning process despises spontaneity and seeks to privilege some at the expense of others. Socialism is premised on support for greed and envy. Hence socialists, when they reject the need for free trade between different countries, are a throwback to pre-modernity and feudalism. Planning on an international scale, even more than is true on a national scale, cannot be anything but a naked rule of force. A failure to appreciate the strengths of the market makes socialism a problematic ideology, strengthening the state, anti-individualism, and an illiberal cultural and political outlook.

Philosophical consequences

The notion that society can be controlled as a whole stems from an archaic animism, a belief that a complex and extended order can somehow be reduced to a 'single purpose'. This is why Hayek argues that socialism is not only factually incorrect, but also logically impossible.

Socialists assume that if there is order, there must be an 'orderer', and they are unable to grasp the fact that order generated without design can far outstrip plans people consciously contrive. Hayek concedes that in small groups like families and tribes, people develop a sense of solidarity and community, and this creates an 'instinctual' belief that we are all the same and must consciously cooperate. This is entirely understandable but it becomes highly problematic when these solidarist instincts (as Hayek calls them) are extended to the wider society, where it is impossible to know individuals.

Fear of the market and abstraction

Competition involves the observance of rules rather than physical force, and so is inevitably abstract. This creates fear and uncertainty among those who fail to see that an extended market order is different in kind from a close-knit small-scale society, and the abstract nature of market relations generates hostility towards money and finance.

When some become wealthy in society, their wealth is ascribed to cheating and exploitation, and there is no understanding that the capitalists are themselves the tools of an impersonal process. They are neither moral nor immoral, since the market itself cannot be characterised in terms appropriate to a small community: moral concepts are irrelevant to questions of competition and the market. Commodities are criticised for what is felt to be the 'artificial' or 'unnatural' character of their value. The moment that barter is replaced by indirect exchange mediated by money, ready intelligibility ceases and abstract interpersonal processes begin that far transcend even the most enlightened individual perception. Money, like sex, simultaneously fascinates, puzzles and repels. The subject bewilders specialists and offends moralists.

The question of religion

Socialists, particularly those of a Marxist persuasion, reject religion and proclaim their atheist credentials. In fact, their real objection to conventional religion is that it challenges the dogma and the 'religion' that they seek to impose upon society.

The idea that all order is by design is an old theological prejudice and instead of a supernatural creator, socialists sometimes substitute the will of a leader or guru, like Marx, Stalin or Mao. Anti-socialists dislike the very term 'social' since the word is often used to suggest that what has been brought about by impersonal and spontaneous processes of the extended order is actually the result of human design.

Production and technology

Production is seen as a physical process: you produce something that is tangible and can be directly experienced. Socialists subscribe to the prejudice that trading is not real work, and adopt what is in reality a medieval notion that it is wicked for money to produce money.

Prices should be 'just' and there is strong intellectual and cultural resistance to the view that the market is a morally indifferent way of allocating its parts. The idea that the market determines the reward is seen as soulless and immoral, and the notion that trade actually creates the very possibility of physical production is deemed contrary to this simplistic version of common sense.

It is not true that technical discoveries in themselves generate wealth. Technological advances have to be fed into a market system so that the new goods and services are traded. The fate of traditional Chinese civilisation is a case in point. Although China had invented gunpowder long before Europe, a feudal mentality led to governmental suppression of the market and merchants, so that inevitably China fell behind Europe.

Liberalism may be Western in origin, but the dramatic changes in Asia (and China itself) demonstrate that markets are by no means a Western phenomenon, and it is part of the demagoguery to which some third world dictators resort, that liberal values are seen as foreign and imperialistic in character. On the contrary: it is socialist values that impede growth and generate backwardness.

Conclusion

The critics of socialism argue that it is a throwback to the middle ages and that it places the community above the individual. The attempt to plan the economy is always disastrous, and has illiberal political and social consequences. Socialism projects an ethic that derives from archaic tribal communities and is quite unsuited to a modern world. The notion that society can be directed and controlled expresses an animistic belief in a unifying purpose that leads to autocracy, a fear of the market and highly simplistic views of the production process.

Summary

- Critics of socialism argue that the planning process inevitably leads to anomaly and distortion, since individual planners seek to gauge the actions and reactions of millions of people.
- Competition necessarily creates winners and losers, and fair competition is secured not by suppressing the market, but through the rule of law and state policies that protect and encourage individual responsibility and initiative.
- Democracy is to be welcomed if it strengthens free enterprise — it is not always positive. Socialists make the mistake of placing the community and the state above the individual and hence act in ways that undermine spontaneity and the individual.
- Philosophically, socialists believe that society can be ordered and designed, and it is not surprising that leadership cults (even in ostensibly atheist societies) are seen to embody a belief in 'society' or the 'nation'.
- Socialists fear the market and have a medieval attitude towards prices and production. They do not understand the importance of trade and the importance of linking technology to the market.

Task 6.1

Read the passage below and answer the question that follows.

Margaret Thatcher's view of socialism

Margaret Thatcher acknowledged that the Second World War (when she was a student) had helped to accustom people to a socialist outlook. They had experienced a centralised economy, and not only were the Conservatives in coalition with Labour, but Labour had tended to preoccupy itself with domestic issues. The 1944 Employment White Paper had committed the Conservatives to full employment (and therefore in Thatcher's view, interference with the market), a massive house rebuilding programme and the creation of a National Health Service. Churchill's comment that socialism required a Gestapo to implement the programme struck her as electorally unwise.

Margaret Thatcher in 1979

When Thatcher became leader of the Conservatives in 1975, the *Daily Telegraph* commented (5 February 1975) that unlike traditional Conservative leaders, she had no

Task 6.1 (continued)

guilt about inherited wealth or privilege, and therefore would not hesitate robustly to defend capitalism against socialism. 'Her accession to the leadership', the paper predicted, 'could mark a sea-change in the whole character of the party political debate in this country.' She liked Keith Joseph's remark that the whole of postwar politics had become a 'socialist racket'. The Tories, she complained, had loosened the corset of socialism: they never removed it. She was opposed to state subsidies and she argued that it was futile and counterproductive for the state to direct investment. This, she argued, merely resulted in ever lower returns on capital.

In *The Downing Street Years* (1983) Thatcher comments pithily that to cure the British disease with socialism was like trying to cure leukaemia with leeches. During her period of office, Hayek was knighted; wholesale privatisation took place; exchange controls were lifted; the trade unions were 'reformed'; council houses were sold to their tenants; and the term 'capitalism' became respectable once again. She described the free market as 'a vast sensitive nervous system, responding to events and signals all over the world to meet the ever-changing needs of peoples in different countries, from different classes, of different religions, with a kind of benign indifference to their status'.

In seeking to smash the state socialism 'in our midst', Thatcher concerned herself not only with public policies but with a change of psychology so that individuals became more assertive and independent minded. Her comment that there is 'no such thing as society' has, she insists, been misunderstood. Her point is that people must look to themselves first. 'It's our duty to look after ourselves and then to look after our neighbour.' Society is not an abstraction but 'a living structure of individuals, families, neighbours and voluntary associations'. Society should not be treated as an excuse — a collectivist escape from individual woes. 'It was a source of obligation.' When Thatcher fell from office in 1990, the centre of political gravity in British society had, it has been argued, shifted rightwards. Socialists were henceforth much more defensive, and the cause of the free market had received a vital boost.

Question

Positive and negative features of 'Thatcherism': which of the following propositions would you endorse, which would you disagree with, and in both cases, why?

- The traditional welfare state undermines the capacity of people to think for themselves and spend their money as they wish.
- Capitalism is a system that gives people freedom and encourages them to take risks and innovate.

Task 6.1 (continued)

- Under free enterprise, people with energy and flair come to the top while those who fail have only themselves to blame.
- Conservative governments since the war were too concerned about consensus politics and were afraid to appear dogmatic and confident of their correctness.
- People who act in antisocial ways should be severely punished. They are to blame for their actions, not their environment.
- Britain can be great again provided it stands up for itself and does not worry too much about what others think of it.
- Trade unionist leaders should be made much more accountable to their members rather than treated as partners who should be consulted by government.
- People who work hard should expect to enjoy the fruits of their labours without interference from the state.
- The market is the fairest and most efficient institution for allocating rewards.

Task 6.2

Using this chapter and other resources available to you, answer the following questions:

1 Is the implementation of an economic plan incompatible with freedom and democracy?
2 Do you see socialism as a dangerously utopian doctrine?
3 'Only the free market can solve humanity's problems.' Discuss.
4 Was Thatcher right to be anxious about what she saw as the socialist character of postwar policies in Britain?
5 'Thatcherism changed British politics for ever.' Do you agree?

Guidance
Question 1
Planning, its critics argue, assumes that the actions of millions of people can be predicted and controlled. It necessarily gives politicians and bureaucrats power to make decisions that backfire, and leads to secrecy and privilege. Planners are conscious of the fact that their policies are inefficient and counterproductive, so that they become tempted to prevent their critics from pointing to their failures and they invent their 'successes' through phoney statistics. The state becomes invested with a godlike character, and planners abuse their powers to secure compliance from powerful groups in society. It becomes tempting to control the media, manipulate the education system and undermine democracy. Attitudes that make sense for small

Task 6.2 (continued)

groups — like solidarity and community — are inappropriate when complex societies, consisting of millions of people, are governed.

It is true that planning can be dictatorial and bureaucratic, but does it have to be like this? Supporters of planning argue that the market can centralise as well as decentralise, and private power can be accumulated that is as much a threat to freedom and democracy as an overweening state. Planners can be sensitive to public opinion provided that liberal institutions are maintained and experts are held account-able to electorates. People have far more skill and insight than they are often given credit for, and the democratic planner needs to listen to groups of citizens when policies are devised to coordinate growth and development. Of course, there is a difference between the solidarity of small groups and the values of complex and populous societies. But there are also similarities. If the media can persuade people to buy goods, they can also invite them to comment on policy initiatives, and encourage a capacity to see the fortunes and wellbeing of others as organically linked to their own.

Question 2

Socialism is an ideology that emphasises cooperation, equality, community and positive freedom. It acknowledges that these values are often disregarded by people, but socialists believe that human nature is not static, it can be changed. It is utopian if by utopia is meant the postulating of an alternative to the present, but this utopia is not dangerous if it is pursued in three ways.

First, socialists need to respect liberal values and institutions. They must build upon the liberal tradition, not reject it, and this means supporting elections even when they lose them, and allowing a free press and freedom of speech, even though things might be printed or said that they do not like and that they find hurtful, even insulting. Second, socialists must be patient. Changing human nature is a long process and socialists must avoid short cuts that artificially accelerate progress. The third way stems from the recognition that an alternative society is not some kind of problem-free promised land, but a step forward along a road that is infinitely long. It is presumptuous and dangerous to imagine that people of today have all the answers. If utopianism is premised on support for liberal values, is patient, humble and respectful, then it is a salutary part of progress and not a dangerous doctrine. Socialists have acted in harmful and damaging ways when they have departed from these three principles.

Question 3

It is certainly true that the free market has made an enormous contribution to human progress. It has made it possible for people to see themselves as individuals, and has

Task 6.2 (continued)

introduced into political vocabulary the notion not only of freedom, but of equality as well. Societies that suppress the free market are inevitably autocratic and inefficient, arrogant and repressive.

But it does not follow from this that the free market is an unblemished institution that deserves our wholehearted support. The free market can generate enormous inequalities, allowing unscrupulous and wealthy individuals to flourish at the expense of honest and poorer ones. The idea that only the state is arbitrary and repressive is a myth. The free market, left to its own devices, divides society and destroys communities. By elevating the individual above society and assuming that there is some kind of natural harmony between the partial interests and the interests of the whole, the free market makes it more difficult to implement the kind of policies that will preserve the environment and encourage people to act responsibly. The free market today has become as much a part of the problem as it is of the solution, and where the market fails to secure human needs there is a case for going beyond it with public institutions based upon discussion and accountability.

Question 4

It is certainly true that all parts of the political spectrum — socialists, conservatives and liberals — believed traditionally that politics was a question of doing things for people, rather than helping them to help themselves. Politicians saw themselves as elitists, doing good for people in a way that can only be described as paternalistic and patronising. This elitism blighted socialist attitudes as well as liberal and conservative ones, and the Fabians in Britain saw themselves as experts whose role was to help the poor and the inarticulate. The National Heath Service, admirable as that institution is, has traditionally treated the suffering as passive victims rather than as adult partners, and local authorities saw the recipients of public housing as 'failures' who needed strict instructions as to what they could and could not do. So Thatcher clearly had a point: people should be encouraged to help themselves.

But two critical points can be raised against the proposition above. The first is that paternalism was not peculiar to the socialists. Liberals and conservatives also adopted elitist attitudes and it would be wrong to suggest that this was the particular prerogative of socialists. Second, it is quite misleading to suggest that paternalism is inherent in socialism. It is true that socialists have been, and often still are, rather authoritarian in their attitudes, but it could be argued that this discredits socialism and works against the emancipatory thrust of socialist policies. How can people govern their own lives if there is some benevolent politician telling them what to do? Socialism cannot be fully democratic if leaders and experts act in autocratic ways, however well intentioned they may be.

Task 6.2 (continued)

Question 5

Supporters of Thatcher argue that the centre of gravity in the British political spectrum shifted rightwards as a result of her premiership. Capitalism and the market became respectable institutions again, and people were now more assertive and entrepreneurial. They felt comfortable about making money and, rather than feeling guilty about their success, they would encourage others to emulate their example. Instead of looking to the society, and the state in particular, for help, individuals were to stand on their own two feet, and take responsibility for their lives. Even post-Thatcher governments, like New Labour under Tony Blair, have been influenced by the ethos of Thatcher's ideas and some of Blair's critics describe him as a 'Thatcherite' rather than as a democratic socialist.

On the other hand, much of British politics in the 1990s, and now in the twenty-first century, has been concerned with undoing Thatcher's legacy. Society rather than the individual is stressed — state intervention highly prized — and while the market is seen as important, the notion that it has all the answers is increasingly rejected as 'market fundamentalism', a dogma as damaging to the community as earlier forms of paternalism were to the individual. New Labour's concept of the 'third way' seeks to combine what are seen as the virtues of Thatcherism — assertiveness, autonomy, a willingness to criticise and question — without the vices — dogma, harshness, abstract individualism. Thatcherism has changed British politics, but not necessarily in ways of which Thatcher herself approves.

Useful websites

- www.hayek.org.uk
- www.margaretthatcher.org/

Further reading

- Hayek, F. A. (1963) *The Constitution of Liberty*, Routledge & Kegan Paul.
- Hayek, F. A. (1979) *The Road to Serfdom*, Routledge & Kegan Paul.
- Hayek, F. A. (1988) *The Fatal Conceit*, Routledge.
- Thatcher, M. (1993) *The Downing Street Years*, Harper Collins.

Is there a case for socialism?

Socialism can only be rescued if we find a way of overcoming both the weaknesses of Marxism and the deficiencies of the social democratic heritage. Communism leads to authoritarianism. This is not simply because Communist Party states developed in what might be called unpropitious circumstances, but because Marxism itself contains 'pre-liberal' features that necessarily generate dogma and dictatorial tendencies.

On the other hand, traditional social democracy is too uncritical of capitalism and the state, and ends up with a dogmatic and passive attitude towards existing realities. In its anxiety to appear 'realistic' and 'constitutional' it tends to accept liberal democracy in ways that do not do sufficiently address inequalities and concentrations of power.

The notion of revolution

Social democrats are surely right to reject the concept of revolution as a dramatic element focused around a seizure of power. It is true that Marx uses the term revolution in different ways. He and Engels speak in the *Communist Manifesto* of the constant 'revolutionising of production' under capitalism and in that sense, revolutions are occurring all the time. But the term revolution is also used to denote a transformation of state and class power — an event in which the character of society as a whole changes.

Marx was to argue that such an event did not have to be violent, and he even took the view in 1882 that if in Britain 'the unavoidable evolution' turned into a revolution, that would not only be the fault of the ruling classes but also of the working class. Every peaceful concession has been wrung out through pressure, and the workers must wield their power and use their liberties, 'both of which they possess legally'. This suggests that each step forward is a kind of revolution in its own right, and that the notion of revolution as a dramatic event, which inevitably changes the character of society, is redundant.

Revolution and authoritarianism

Marx, however, generally viewed revolution as a dramatic event linked to a seizure of power. This idea was, it seems to me, inherited uncritically from the French Revolution of 1789. It creates a polarisation that makes the assertion of common interests and consensus more, not less, difficult.

Engels was right: revolutions are authoritarian events, which create a new state that has to differentiate between revolutionaries and counter-revolutionaries, and this leads to the kind of insecurity and division that generates despotism rather than democracy. If the notion of revolution as inevitable creates the problem of supporting revolutions that generate authoritarian states and the consequent abuse of human rights, a scathing attitude towards morality can only aggravate the problem. But it does not follow from this that all elements of Marxism are authoritarian in orientation.

Here the attitude towards liberalism is crucial. Not only did Marx begin his political career as a liberal steeped in the ideals of the European Enlightenment, but when he became a Communist he sought to go beyond, rather than reject, liberal values.

Transcending, as opposed to rejecting, liberalism

The distinction between 'transcending' and 'rejecting' liberalism is crucial to my argument. To transcend liberalism is to build upon its values and institutions: it is to develop a theory and practice that extends freedom and equality more consistently and comprehensively than liberalism is able to do.

Socialism as a 'postliberalism' seeks to turn liberal values into concrete realities so that those excluded by classical liberalism — the workers, the poor, women, dependents — become free and equal, as part of a historical process that has no grand culminating moment or climax. Socialism as a 'pre-liberalism', on the other hand, negates liberal values by introducing a system that imposes despotic controls upon the population at large (whatever its claim to speak in the name of the workers), and it is well described in the *Communist Manifesto* as a reactionary socialism because it hurls 'traditional anathemas' against liberalism and representative government.

The amalgam of pre- and postliberalism

Marxism is an amalgam of preliberalism and postliberalism. It is postliberal in so far as it stresses the need to build upon, rather than reject, capitalist achievements. (Conventionally defined) revolutions make sense in situations in which legal rights to change society are blocked, but in societies that have, or are attempting to build, liberal institutions, revolutions lead to elitism, despotism and a contempt for democracy.

The notion of class war does not place enough emphasis on the need to create and consolidate common interests, to campaign in a way that isolates those who oppose progress. Moreover, there is a tension in Marx's writings between his view that a classless society will eliminate alienation for all, and his argument that the bourgeoisie are the 'enemy' who must be overthrown. The latter leads to the privileging of the proletariat as the agent of revolution, and hostility to all who are not proletarians.

Social democrats are right to reject the need for revolution (at least in liberal societies where adults have political rights): socialism can only be democratic if it is evolutionary in character.

Class and agency

Socialists are correct to see class as something that is negative; freedom for all, as Marxism argues, is only possible in a classless society. Class privileges some at the expense of others. In liberal societies it encourages an abstract approach to be taken to equality and power so that formal equality coexists with the most horrendous inequalities of power and material resources. Class is thus divisive, and it generates the kind of antagonisms that require force (and therefore the state) to tackle them.

For this reason Marx can be defended when he contends that if we want to dispense with the need for an institution claiming a monopoly of legitimate force (i.e. the state), we must dispense with classes. Marx argues that in class-divided societies, social relations are not 'relations between individual and individual, but between worker and capitalist, between farmer and landlord etc. Wipe out these relations and you annihilate all society'.

But this comment is not concrete enough. For workers also have a gender and national identity etc., and this materially affects how they relate to others. It is not that the class identity is unimportant: it is rather that it fuses with other identities since these other identities are also a crucial part of the process that creates class. 'Racial', religious, ethnic, national and sexual identities (to name just a few) are not unimportant: the point is that we do not need to present these other identities as though they are separate from class.

The importance of form

Class, in my view, is only seen in 'other' forms. Thus we are told (in the *Independent*, 8 May 2003) that whereas 4.5% of white British men (age 16–74) are unemployed, this figures rises to 9.1% for men of Pakistani origin, 10.2% of Bangladeshis and 10.4% of Afro-Caribbean men. There are not simply two sets of figures here (black and Asian men and unemployment); rather, it is that unemployment is integral to the discrimination from which black and Asian men suffer.

Class only becomes visible through the position of women, gay people, ethnic minorities etc. The diversity of form in which classes express themselves is of the utmost importance, and it is the reason why no particular group should be privileged over any other in the struggle to achieve a classless and stateless society.

Support for socialism

Socialists must, as I see it, seek to mobilise all those who are excluded by contemporary institutions. This goes well beyond the concept of a 'proletariat', although those who are poor and have to subject themselves to the 'despotic' rules of employers (where the latter act in an authoritarian way) are an obvious constituency in the struggle to govern one's own life.

It is impossible to be free and equal if one is subject to aggressive pressures from employers and managers. Democratising the workplace to allow greater security, transparency and participation is critical, and all those who suffer from these problems are natural constituents in the struggle for socialism.

But the point is that we cannot exclude the wealthy and the 'beneficiaries' of the market and state from the struggle for socialism, even though it would be foolish and naïve to assume that the 'haves' will be enthusiastic proponents for a socialist future! Nevertheless, it has to be said that those who drive cars (however rich they are) are still vulnerable to the health problems associated with pollution. They suffer the nervous disorders linked to congestion and frustration on the roads. Inequalities and lack of social control, whether within or between societies, make everyone insecure and result in a futile and wasteful use of resources. Wealthy people who try to 'buy' peaceful neighbourhoods are seeking to escape from problems that will inevitably affect them too.

The liberal tradition

It is becoming increasingly clear to 'establishments' in advanced industrial countries that if nothing is done about the divisions within the international community, then liberal traditions will be eroded, as refugees move around the globe. We will *all* suffer as a consequence.

The British government recently announced measures to place terrorist suspects under 'house arrest'. Is this simply a matter of concern for 'others'? To take another example: although the victims of crime in, say, contemporary South Africa are predominantly the poor who live in the shanty towns, this scourge does not simply affect those who are on the margins of society. Everyone can be the victim of crime. Socialism — making people conscious that they are living in society and that everything they do affects (and may harm) others — is, it could be argued, in everyone's interests. There is an interesting parallel here with measures taken to combat cholera in nineteenth-century British cities. The disease was no respecter of class or wealth: it was in everyone's interests that it was eradicated. What is the point of having wealth and power if your health is devastated?

Marxists might argue that with divisiveness and inequality throughout the world increasing as the result of capitalism and globalisation, the notion of a proletariat must be viewed internationally rather than simply nationally. But the danger still remains that such a perspective will take a narrow view of class and underplay the problem of cementing common interests across the globe.

Socialism and inevitability

Marx sometimes makes it seem that socialism will arrive come what may. In *Capital* he speaks of 'the natural laws of capitalist production' 'working with iron necessity towards inevitable results', and in a famous passage he likens the birth of socialism to pregnancy. The development of socialism is as inevitable as the birth of a child.

This argument is, however, only defensible when we subscribe to a *conditional* inevitability — not an absolute certainty independent of circumstances. In the *Communist Manifesto*, Marx and Engels comment that class struggle might end in 'a revolutionary constitution of society at large' or in 'the common ruin of the contending classes'. Not only is it impossible to establish a timescale for socialism, but its inevitability is conditional upon, for example, humanity avoiding a nuclear conflagration which wipes out humans, or the destruction of the environment which makes production impossible.

Nor can it be said that liberal societies might not turn to the right before they turn to the left. What the idea of a conditional inevitability implies is that *if* humanity survives, then sooner or later it will have to regulate its affairs in a socially conscious manner and that, broadly speaking, is socialism. Only in this qualified and conditional sense can it be said that socialism is inevitable.

The problem of free will

Marxism can only be rescued if it makes it clear that inevitability is conditional, if it drops a notion of revolution as a concentrated political event, and with it a polarised and narrow notion of class. Whether it would still be Marxism after changes of this kind is a moot point.

In his hostility to utopianism Marx sometimes gives the impression that he does not believe in free will. When he speaks of his theory of history as one in which people enter into relations 'independent of their will', does this mean that people have no will? What it means, it seems to me, is that what people intend (i.e. humans are beings with purpose and thus will) is never quite the same as what actually happens.

Take the following assertion of Marx's: the capitalist and landlord are 'the personifications of economic categories, embodiments of particular class interests and class relations' so that his or her standpoint can 'less than any other' make the individual 'responsible for relations whose creature he socially remains, however much he may subjectively raise himself above them'. This comment seems to suggest that our will cannot transform circumstances, and therefore we cannot create new relations.

A different kind of determinism

Yet Marx's third thesis on Feuerbach had already stated (against mechanical materialism, which saw people as passive and lacking in agency) that the changing of circumstances and human activity coincide as 'revolutionary practice' (again — an identification of revolution with ongoing change, not a dramatic one-off event). This, it seems to us, is the answer to the problem of determinism and inevitability.

If we assume that determinism negates free will and that we need to make a choice between them, then clearly determinism is a problem for socialism. For how can we change society if we do not have the will to do so? But what if we go beyond such a 'dualism' (i.e. an unbridgeable gulf) and argue merely that determinism means that free will always occurs in the context of relations? Why is this concept of determinism a problem?

Circumstances determine our capacities. Our capacity to change circumstances involves recognising these circumstances and making sure that we appraise their reality correctly. To strengthen the struggle for socialism successfully we need to attend to movements within our existing society which demonstrate that we can regulate our lives in ways that increase our capacity to get the results we want — whether it is in terms of transport policy, cleaning up the environment, giving people greater security and control in the workplace etc. Whether these reforms or 'revolutionising activities' are effective depends upon how carefully we have assessed the circumstances that determine the context and the event.

This kind of determinism does not undermine free will: on the contrary, it makes it possible to harness free will in a sensible and rational manner. If Marx was suggesting that there is a 'dualism' between free will and determinism, he would simply be turning classical liberalism inside out and not going beyond it. Classical liberalism argues for a notion of freedom independent of circumstances and relationships, and socialists might find it tempting (since they are critical of liberalism) to take the view that since circumstances determine the way people are, therefore people have no freedom or will power. But if this was the position of socialists like Robert Owen, arguably it was not the position of Marx's 'new' materialism, even though he and Engels sometimes gave the impression that it was.

The weaknesses of Bernstein

A credible socialism must draw upon social democratic *and* Marxist ideas. The problem with 'pure' social democrats as well as 'pure' Marxists is that they can be said to either embrace a (liberal) empiricist framework or to simply turn such a framework inside out.

Bernstein is a case in point. On the one hand, he saw himself as a positivist who stuck rigorously to the facts. On the other, since he was living in a society that was clearly not socialist, socialism is, he tells us, a piece of the beyond — something that ought to be, but is not. Abstract 'realism' coexists with abstract utopianism. The role of ethics is not integrated into a concern with the facts, and Marck has pointed out that such a theory can pay too much attention to 'short-run developments', ruling out in a dogmatic fashion dramatic and unanticipated actions, 'apparently contradicted by the happenings of the day'.

The danger of dogmatism

Bernstein's position on economic concentration suggests that wishful thinking can sometimes blind us to the facts. As Gay comments in his book on Bernstein, after 1924 German industry centralised and cartelised as never before. The trends that he analysed in 1899 were not irreversible. In the same way Bernstein assumed that a new middle class would be democratic and pro-socialist. Yet anyone who knows anything about German history after the First World War, comments Gay, 'will recognise the fallacious assumptions of Bernstein's theory'. Inflation and the world depression traumatised large groups within the German middle classes: they saw descent into the proletariat as a horrendous possibility.

Bernstein's analysis, put into the context of Germany between the wars, turned out to be wishful thinking. Whether government through a representative parliament can work depends upon the social structure and political institutions of a country — it allows of no dogmatic answer.

Utopianism and realism

Once we see that reality is in movement we can fuse utopia and realism. Utopia derives from the transformation of existing realities: but this utopia is not to be located outside existing realities; it is part of them.

In arguing that socialism must be a 'utopian realism' we avoid the dualism between facts and values, utopia and reality, a dualism that bedevils so many exponents of socialism, whether of the right or the left. Bernstein's argument that socialists should always avoid violence is right under some circumstances. But it could hardly apply when the Hitler leadership in Germany destroyed parliamentary institutions and embraced fascism.

We need a state as long as humanity cannot resolve its conflicts of interest in a peaceful manner. For Bernstein, however, because the state exists, it is here to stay! The 'so-called coercive associations, the state and the communities, will retain their great tasks in any future I can see'. But to identify the state with community, and regard its mechanisms for settling difference as only apparently 'coercive', shows how far 'pure' social democracy is still steeped in the abstract aspects of the liberal tradition.

Gay is surely right when he comments that Bernstein's optimism was not well founded: it took short-run prosperity and converted it into a law of capitalist development. If, as A. J. P. Taylor has said, Marx was a dogmatic optimist, so was Bernstein. Socialism requires a conditional concept of inevitability and a 'dialectical' determinism — one that takes full account of human agency — so that it is neither 'optimistic' nor 'pessimistic' but is a utopian realism.

Conclusion

A viable notion of socialism is, in my view, only possible if we draw upon both social democratic and Marxist traditions, avoiding the weaknesses and building upon the strengths of each. Marxism has a problematic notion of revolution as a concentrated political event and this goal, if sought in a society with liberal institutions, can only be counterproductive and authoritarian. The notion of class is also too narrow in the classical Marxist tradition. While it is true that class is a barrier to emancipation, the concept must be reconceptualised so that it fuses with gender, religious, regional etc. and other identities. Class does not stand outside these identities: on the contrary, they are the 'forms' through which class expresses itself. The question of inevitability must be seen as conditional in character, not as something built into 'inexorable' historical laws.

If social democrats are right to stress reform rather than revolution (in liberal societies), they also tend to invert the one-sidedness of the Marxist tradition by presenting short-term trends in dogmatic fashion, as though no major change is possible. Socialism can and must appeal to the whole of society (albeit in different ways) and utopianism and realism need to reinforce, rather than work against, one another.

Summary

- The notion of revolution is problematic in Marxism. While we can legitimately speak of revolution as critical change, the idea of revolution as a popular insurrection undermines democracy and polarises society.
- A viable socialism must transcend rather than reject liberalism, and the problem with Marxism is that it incorporates a number of illiberal or pre-liberal ideas that get in the way of emancipation and freedom.
- The concept of class is important but it must be handled concretely so that full account is taken of the way in which people experience oppression and exploitation.

- If socialism is defined as regulating society in people's interests, then its supporters are not confined to the poor or disadvantaged, since all suffer from the stresses and strains imposed by a market society.
- Socialism can only be defined as 'inevitable' if we embrace a conditional notion of inevitability. Determinism does not mean that things happen come what may, but that people's choices will only be successful if they are linked to a hard-headed appraisal of the circumstances acting upon them.
- Marxists can be dogmatic and so too can social democrats. In his anxiety to avoid polarisation and conflict, Bernstein ignored the unpalatable trends developing in his native Germany.
- Utopianism is a valuable part of the socialist tradition provided it is linked to, and firmly rooted in, realities.

Task 7.1

Read the passage below and answer the question that follows.

Blair — socialist or conservative?

The evidence that Blair is not a socialist at all, democratic or Marxist, seems strong. Not only is he public-school educated, but he is comfortable in the company of wealthy business people and has seldom, if ever, attacked the principles of capitalism. Mandelson, a close friend, has stated that 'New Labour is intensely relaxed about people becoming filthy rich'.

Blair, it is argued, has no roots in the Labour Party. His economic policies are seen as blue rather than red: independence for the Bank of England, a curb on public spending, and a refusal to raise the rate of tax. His support for the Iraq War meant aligning himself to a Republican president in the USA. He has failed to reform the House of Lords, continued with the Conservatives' internal market in the National Health Service, and the introduction of foundation hospitals has, critics argue, favoured the successful over the struggling. Private finance initiatives have helped the private sector at the expense of the public sector and targets and league tables have furthered elitism in education, while the proposed introduction of variable fees in universities has discouraged poorer students from attending. In general, Blair, it is said, has moved away from equality as a socialist goal, and since he came to power the rich have got richer and the poor poorer.

On the other hand, defenders of Blair as a socialist argue that he has a modern attitude towards business and is concerned to win the middle classes to progressive positions. The independence of the Bank of England is part of a package of policies that seek to keep the rate of inflation and of unemployment low, and that as far as

Task 7.1 (continued)

the House of Lords is concerned, hereditary peers have virtually been abolished (hardly a Conservative policy).

The war in Iraq follows earlier Labour foreign policy when Labour sided with the USA during the Cold War, and financial initiatives in the health service have resulted in greater efficiency. Cuts in public expenditure were confined to his first 2 years in office and have given way to pledges to spend more, not less. The policies of devolution for Scotland and Wales and the elected mayor for London are hardly Conservative policies, and the introduction of the minimum wage has assisted the low paid. Those on low incomes have also been helped by the 'working person's tax credit', preschool children have been assisted by the Sure Start programme, and his policies have had the effect of slowing down the development of inequality.

A 'troops out of Iraq' demonstration in central London, March 2006

Question

Which of these propositions would you oppose, and which would you support, and why?

- Blair has been a supremely successful politician. He has led the Labour Party to three consecutive electoral victories.
- Blair is an opportunist who has caved in to pressure from big business and failed to carry through policies that protect the weak and the vulnerable.
- Blair is a modern socialist. He is concerned that socialism should be popular and relevant. He is willing to take risks by taking on those he calls 'conservatives' in the

Task 7.2 (continued)

human rights abuses committed in its name, and therefore it can only play a positive role in developing the case for socialism when its weaknesses and deficiencies are tackled and remedied.

Question 2

Social democrats are right to concentrate on practical policies that change people's lives for the better. This means that socialists must not only be a position to implement policies, but they must obtain and maintain power in ways that are seen as legitimate by most members of the community. Social democrats have a positive attitude towards liberals and liberalism, seeking to persuade rather than impose, and acknowledging that all members of society have skills that can contribute to improving society.

On the other hand, there is also truth in the quotation. Like the utopian socialists whom Marx and Engels criticised in the nineteenth century, social democrats have sometimes detached values from historical realities, as though a just society can result simply because people strongly desire its realisation. But whereas these 'utopians' did want a radically different kind of society, social democrats have sometimes been so immersed in the details of particular policies that they have ignored the need to change human beings and take emancipatory values seriously. Social democrats appear, as a consequence, to be almost indistinguishable from liberals and conservatives, so that frustrated socialists turn away from democratic socialism altogether.

Question 3

The notion of inevitability must be handled with extreme care. The idea that socialism is inevitable can lead to arrogance and a false sense of certainty. The importance of long-term objectives is used to squeeze out a concern with everyday life and a belief that whatever happens contributes to this long-term inevitability and should be accepted as a result. A kind of dogmatic optimism results that can mean that the daily problems of real people are brushed aside: debates become unnecessary and alternative points of view pilloried and their upholders persecuted.

The notion of inevitability can play a positive role if it is handled with humility and sensitivity. In the first place, it is quite wrong to think that socialism will arrive come what may. If humanity is destroyed through a nuclear holocaust or our capacity to produce and reproduce ruined through an irresponsible attitude to the environment, then there will be no socialism. A viable notion of inevitability has to be a conditional concept: whether socialism is inevitable depends upon whether humanity itself survives. There is no god-given certainty that it will necessarily triumph. On the other hand, we are becoming more and more conscious of how interdependent society is, and that individual wellbeing is only possible if we contribute to, and see ourselves as

Task 7.1 (continued)

Labour movement — those who live in the past and ignore the need for innovation and change.

- Blair is not a socialist, but a Tory who treats the Labour Party with contempt. His belief that he is right shows a tendency to authoritarianism, and a supine attitude to the powers that be.
- Blair has shown a willingness to be tough in the view he takes of terrorism and the support that he has given for the US 'war on terror'. His policies have been courageous, and he believes that it is important to be moral and do what you believe is right, even if this is controversial and provokes opposition in some quarters.
- Blair's support for the US administration, and his decision to send troops to Iraq, has been disastrous. Large swathes of public opinion oppose him, and he will be remembered negatively as a result of a failure to conduct British policies in an independent and considered fashion.

Task 7.2

Using this chapter and resouces available to you, answer the following questions:

1 Does Marxism have any role to play in making the case for socialism?
2 Is it fair to characterise social democracy as a 'utopian socialism minus utopian expectations'?
3 Is socialism inevitable?
4 Is social-ism the same as socialism?
5 Is it possible to develop a form of socialism that is neither authoritarian nor opportunist?

Guidance

Question 1

Marxism has an important part to play in developing a viable form of socialism. It is critical of class divisions and identifies an emancipated society as one that is both classless and without a state. It seeks to address general questions of history (even nature, some argue), so that it is a world outlook and not simply a particular set of policy prescriptions. It invites us to look beyond a capitalist society based on the market to one in which people enjoy working, have security and respect one another.

On the other hand, Marxism has also done huge damage to the socialist movement. It has encouraged arrogance and divisiveness, and proved to be attractive to those seeking change from above. Marxism cannot simply be exonerated for the

Task 7.2 (continued)

part and parcel of, society itself. Trade, technological advance and production are increasingly stitching the world together, and this creates a basis for the development of the idea that we are part of a wider community. Individual freedom must be seen in terms of how we develop the lives of others and the lives of ourselves — this is inevitable in the sense that if we are to flourish, a greater sense of public awareness and sensitive public regulation must increase.

Question 4

The understanding that we are individuals who form relations with others and ourselves lies at the heart of socialism. Being aware of our membership of society is a necessary, but not sufficient, condition for a viable democratic socialism. Community consciousness can be repressive and stifling unless the people belonging to a community see themselves as independent and critical individuals. Socialism arose historically out of the inadequacies of an individualism that allowed some to flourish at the expense of others, and socialism can only retain its democratic credentials if socialist institutions are concerned with the development of all human beings. Social-ism is the same as socialism, if by this we mean institutions and policies that promote our understanding that everything we do affects others, and therefore we have a responsibility to ensure that this impact is as positive and empowering as possible.

On the other hand, this social awareness can seem vague and unanchored unless we address the question of capitalism and the market. Entrepreneurship and risk taking are positive provided they embrace everyone and are genuinely developmental in character. Inequalities prevent people from putting themselves in one another's position. Wealth and ownership must be related to needs, and needs are not simply desires: they are desires that develop us positively, not negatively — that enrich and do not destroy life. Socialism must address problems of health, education, housing, leisure etc. in ways that are practical and effective. Socialist values need organisational teeth, enabling people to cooperate, respect one another and flourish both collectively and individually. Social awareness is not itself socialist if it leads to division, force and inequality.

Question 5

Socialists must not blame others for problems that can be laid at their own door. They need to understand why socialists in the past have either been authoritarian or opportunist so that they can avoid these kinds of mistake in the future.

Authoritarian socialism arises out of an impatience with capitalism that leads to short cuts and fictional solutions. Utopianism is positive if it projects an alternative to the present: it becomes negative if it ignores contemporary realities and allows

Task 7.2 (continued)

wishful thinking to dominate instead. We often think of romanticism as an other-worldly, somewhat indulgent view of life, harmless and temporary. But romanticism can be much more sinister than this if it leads political movements to believe that rapid and wholesale change can be imposed upon society through a dedicated elite committed to their cause, and willing to use violence to achieve their ends.

Socialists need to respect and work with people, understanding their problems and encouraging them to see the positive and critical implications of their own positions. But abandoning the notion of revolution is no good if it leads to a fear of change itself; capitalism and the market are tenacious but they are not eternal — they developed historically, they are continually changing and it is crucial to avoid replacing negative dogmas with positive ones. Realism requires that we see the world as dynamic and not static, so that we embrace liberal values while remaining conscious of their historical drawbacks. We can only develop a socialism that is neither authoritarian nor opportunist if we avoid veering from one extreme to another. We must continuously ask critical questions about force, inequality and exploitation while being aware that these problems have been around for a long time. The problem with magical solutions is that they not only fail, but lead to a kind of disillusionment that then undermines any attempt to make the world a better place.

Useful websites

- www.the-wood.org/socialism/
- www.marxist.org.uk/htm_docs/princip2.htm

Further reading

- Gay, P. (1962) *The Dilemma of Democratic Socialism*, Collier Books.
- Hoffman, J. (1975) *Marxism and the Theory of Praxis*, Lawrence & Wishart.
- Hoffman, J. and Graham, P. (2006) *Introduction to Political Ideologies*, Pearson Longman.
- Marx, K. (1863) *Capital*, Vol. 1, Progress, 1970.
- Marx, K. and Engels, F. (1967) *The Communist Manifesto*, with introduction by A. J. P. Taylor, Penguin, 1967.
- Marx, K. and Engels, F. (1975) *Selected Correspondence*, Progress.

Conclusion

One of the problems of getting to grips with socialism is the number of different forms that it can take. It is hardly surprising that Wright calls his book *Socialisms*, but socialism, though variegated, can be defined. What do all socialisms have in common?

They are all uneasy about capitalism; they all support cooperation (having an optimistic view of human nature); they regard freedom as a question of resources and not just one of rights; and they all subscribe to some notion of equality.

Utopianism

Socialism is vulnerable to the charge raised by its critics that it is utopian (in the sense of seeking a society that exists nowhere) and, it is argued, this makes it prone to authoritarianism. By stressing its commitment to equality as some kind of ideal we can differentiate socialism from doctrines and movements that have sometimes claimed to be 'socialistic' (think of the concept of 'national socialism' or Nazism) but which are hostile to notions of freedom and equality.

One way around the problem of utopianism is to regard other socialisms as utopian, but your own as 'scientific'. Marxism adopts this strategy, but it is open to two objections. The first is that many socialists in the nineteenth century considered themselves scientific, including writers like Saint-Simon, Fourier and Owen, whom Marx and Engels labelled as utopian. Second, the question can well be posed: what is wrong with utopia in the sense of projecting a rather different set of social arrangements from those that exist at present?

The question is not whether a theory is utopian, but whether its alternative is viable or purely fantastic. Not surprisingly, Marx and Engels drew upon the ideas of those whom they spoke of rather scornfully as 'utopian'. Moreover, there is a major problem with Marxism's 'scientific' features. They move the theory of socialism away from democracy and help to explain why Marxist societies have been highly authoritarian in practice.

The inevitability problem

Take the concept that socialism is inevitable. Marxists regard this concept as taking socialism out of the realm of the 'desirable' so that, like an earthquake, it is simply unavoidable. This argument creates all kinds of problems. It suggests that any kind of 'upheaval' should be supported since it is 'on the way' to creating the conditions for socialism. As a result, socialists give adherence to systems and regimes that may discredit their values.

Rosa Luxemburg, the Polish revolutionary, felt obliged to support the heroic endeavours of the Russian Bolsheviks (as she saw them) even though she deplored the authoritarianism of Lenin and Trotsky. Marx, as president of the First International, showered praise upon the Paris Commune although privately he expressed grave reservations about its formation.

Authoritarianism can be reinforced by a notion of class struggle as 'war', and a belief that socialism is scientifically 'necessary' rather than ethically desirable may lead to a casual attitude towards moral principles. The problem of leadership that exists in all emancipatory political movements becomes particularly acute when linked to these aspects of 'scientific socialism'.

The dilemma of democratic socialism

All this suggests that democratic socialism or social democracy is preferable to Marxism. Certainly it is true that social democracy rejects Marxist arguments even though, in the case of Bernstein's pioneering critique, an evolutionary socialism is presented as the kind of socialism that, it is argued, Marx himself would have embraced had he lived later and seen the way that history and society developed.

Social democrats have their own problems, however. By rejecting Marxism so absolutely, they can become difficult to distinguish from liberals and one-nation conservatives (a problem graphically exemplified by Tony Blair's socialism), and this leads to the argument that social democracy is a movement away from, rather than a sensible embodiment of, socialism.

The British Labour Party

No analysis of democratic socialism would be complete without some account of the British Labour Party, since the latter demonstrates in its practice the pragmatism, empiricism and gradualism of social democratic principles. Indeed,